WALKING WITH COSMIC DANCER JOSEPH RAEL

MARY ELIZABETH MARLOW

Pointer Oak / Tri S Foundation

Distributed by Millichap Books

© 2017 Mary Elizabeth Marlow. All rights reserved

Artworks © 2015 Joseph Rael

First edition. First printing
Book and jacket design by Carl Brune
Printed in USA

ISBN 978-1-937462-40-6

millichapbooks.com

WHAT IS A COSMIC DANCER?

SOME MEETINGS ARE DIVINE APPOINTMENTS. Such was the case with my first encounter with Joseph Rael (Beautiful Painted Arrow).

As he prepared to conduct a sweat lodge, Joseph took a walk down a path in the woods and stopped dead-still as he approached me coming from the opposite direction. We looked intently at each other. It was a sacred moment. A timeless moment. No words were spoken, yet a great deal was communicated. Sometime later, Joseph said he was seeing my entire future in *slices* of light. These bursts of energy are similar to what quantum physicists call "quanta," a light not visible to the untrained mind.

Seeing in slices of light? *Really?* This was not familiar to me, but it was a preview of what was to come as he helped me gradually shift from the limited mind and tap into the Higher Mind with infinite possibilities.

A Pueblo Indian of the Picuris and Ute tribes, a mystic and visionary, Joseph Rael came to Virginia Beach in 1983 to conduct a sweat lodge ceremony and a weekend seminar. I knew little about him but I was curious, so I signed up to participate in the sweat lodge. This man is a keeper of ancient wisdom. He has the soul of a mystic, one who has merged with the heart of God. Joseph is a cosmic dancer, a multidimensional being whose dance in life is choreographed by universal consciousness. At the time, I could not foresee the significance of our meeting or the series of precipitous events which would unfold several years later to draw us back together again.

CONTENTS

PROLOGUE : REMARKABLE MEETING ········· vii

CHAPTER ONE : LISTENING IS GIVING ············· 1

CHAPTER TWO : METAPHORS ARE THE LANGUAGE
                OF UNIVERSAL CONSCIOUSNESS ········ 13

CHAPTER THREE : ALL CEREMONIES REFLECT
                  THE DESIRE TO GET IN TOUCH
                  WITH HIGHER MIND ········· 23

CHAPTER FOUR : CEREMONIAL DANCE
                EXPANDS OUR BEING ············ 33

CHAPTER FIVE : FEMININE ENERGY COMES FIRST:
                THE MASCULINE IS AN EXTENSION
                OF THE FEMININE ············ 41

CHAPTER SIX : WE ARE NOT HERE ············ 49

CHAPTER SEVEN : DON'T GET STUCK IN FORM ········· 55

CHAPTER EIGHT : WHAT WE THINK WE KNOW
                 IS NOT WHAT IS ············ 65

CHAPTER NINE : LIVE INSIDE DIVINE PRESENCE ········· 71

CHAPTER TEN : FALL IN LOVE WITH LIFE ········· 81

NOTES   91
ACKNOWLEDGEMENTS   93
ABOUT THE AUTHOR   95

PROLOGUE

REMARKABLE MEETING

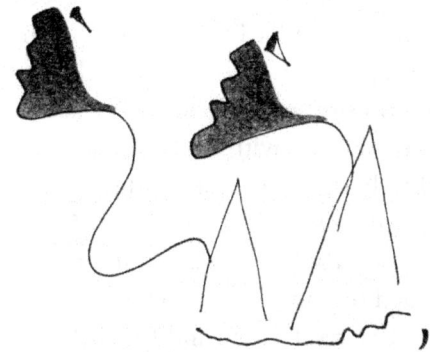

AFTER THE SWEAT LODGE, MY SON JOHN STAYED FOR THE TEACH-INGS ON THE MEDICINE WHEEL. When I returned to pick him up, he mentioned that Joseph had invited him to Colorado to watch him and others perform the Sun Dance Ceremony.

I had a short discussion with Joseph about the offer. Since I knew almost nothing about the Sun Dance, the possibility of allowing a fourteen-year-old to go with mostly strangers to an unfamiliar place and experience something totally unknown to me, was simply not an option. Had I known then what I know now, I would have seen this as the opportunity of a lifetime and would have immediately said yes. After that weekend, there was no mention of Joseph in the circles in which I traveled.

Five years later, a group of Houston women wanted Native American teachings to be included in our upcoming yearly retreat. The suggestion was a good one since we had decided to convene in Santa Fe. It also meant the need to find someone who could teach the Native American portion of our retreat. I just assumed the right person would somehow show up.

Some days later, Sally Perry, a Virginia Beach friend, invited me to a party for Joseph Rael. It was a large festive gathering primarily for those who had some prior connection to Joseph's teachings. Upon arrival at the gathering, Joseph and I exchanged cordial greetings. That was that. No other conversations between the two of us ensued during the evening, though I did spend time talking at length with Peggy, his partner.

The next evening there was another invitation to join with a circle of friends (including Joseph and Peggy) for a special showing of a documentary film on the East Indian mystic, Meher Baba. After the film, this same group went out to dinner. Halfway through the meal, I turned to the person sitting beside me and mentioned I had "put out in spirit for someone to teach with." The request was not specifically for someone versed in Native American traditions, rather a teaching partner in a much broader context. I had just completed thirteen-years co-teaching with the late Paul Solomon, an international teacher of esoteric wisdom. It included teaching on my own as well as co-teaching with Paul in the United States, Europe and Israel. All in all it was a wonderful experience. I was eager to teach with someone else in a similar fashion.

Meanwhile, sitting directly across from me at the circular table was Joseph Rael. Apparently, I was in total disconnect. It never occurred to me that the person I was prayerfully inviting to enter my life just might be Joseph.

Destiny Intervenes

Because I was missing what was right in front of me, destiny intervened. That night my dream indicated Joseph and I would be working together. I was stunned. The next morning an early morning phone call came from Peggy. They had been scheduled to leave that morning by plane, but all flights had been cancelled because Virginia Beach was snowbound. That in itself was unusual. After all, Virginia Beach is a resort city in the southeast corner of Virginia. Sand and sun prevail, not snow. Had it not been for the extreme weather, would I ever have walked with and learned so much from Joseph? An interesting thought to ponder.

"Hon," began Peggy, "I think you're supposed to be teaching with Joseph. Why don't you come and join a group of us for dinner tonight?" Once again on this third evening (three being the number of resolution and completion) life placed me with Joseph. This time the group gathered at a restaurant where Joseph was seated far away from me on the other side of a long rectangular table. So again, no words—just a smile and a nod. After dinner, we went back to Sally Perry's home where conversations with others continued.

Finally, Sally (who often serves as a catalyst for change) said in an all-knowing, straightforward manner, "Mary Elizabeth, aren't you supposed to be talking to Joseph about teaching with him?" Wasting no more time, I quickly walked across the room and sat cross-legged on the rug in front of Joseph, who was sitting comfortably in a chair. Immediately, he got up from his chair and positioned himself on the floor facing me. It was a gracious gesture of meeting on the same level.

"Joseph, I'm planning to give a retreat program in New Mexico this summer. Our group is eager to learn something about Native American teachings. Would you be willing to share some of your wisdom with this group?"

He looked directly into my eyes, listened intently and answered with a simple, "Yes." There were no questions, no discussion of details of any kind. That's it? It was the end of our "talk." As I would continue to learn over the years, though Joseph often speaks in his own unique poetic prose, he is also a person who doesn't rely solely on words for communication. It is what some native people call *high* language, a spiritual language where one sees, knows, and senses non-verbally.

Our coming together seemed an unlikely match, at least from a logical perspective. We differ in many ways: in background, education, culture, and mores. I enjoy the comforts of the modern world, love the arts, follow fashion, appreciate good food (a "foodie" at heart) and prefer high thread-count bedsheets. In addition, I knew almost nothing about the Native American traditions and am directionally impaired. None of the above mentioned are exactly native traits.

On the other hand, as a child I was allowed to spend countless hours outdoors to run, play, create, and imagine all kinds of games and scenarios with the children in our neighborhood. In addition there was the freedom to explore the ever unfolding wonders of life on our farm and enjoy the winding paths and natural beauty of the nearby Blue Ridge Mountains. Thank goodness I was allowed to be a child and develop a curious and adventuresome spirit. Without those experiences, my journey with Joseph may have been short-lived.

Our coming together may have been one of the above reasons or something totally different. Once, while sitting with Joseph at the kitchen table in my home, he asked. "Who is the Native American woman who stands smiling behind you?" I quickly said, "It must be Corrine, the Seneca Indian woman who took care of me when I was very young."

"I knew there must have been someone in your early years who had a strong influence on you."

Memories of Corrine: tall, beautiful, high cheek bones, and smiling eyes are still vivid. Could it be the vibration she emanated was so deeply encoded that years later, when Joseph and the Native ways arrived on the scene, mysterious chords of memory were stirred—and a recognition and familiarity of something loving and beautiful rose to the surface?

When Joseph agreed to teach with me, I assumed it would be for just that one program. As it turned out, we taught together for ten years. During that time, we each had our own pursuits and would come together to teach mostly in Colorado and New Mexico, though we also co-taught in Virginia, England and Norway. Topics included vision quests, metaphoric mind, mysteries of the dance, sacred sites and ceremonies, rites of passage, and many others. We also collaborated on a book entitled *Being and Vibration*.

"I can still see you in my minds eye in Bernalillo that morning after everyone left and we three could visit. I think you're a special person to do things with us, so let's workout some other contribution or wrkshops, etc."

PROLOGUE

The Sound/Peace Chamber

A few weeks later, when Joseph and I finally talked together on the phone, we agreed to get together before the August retreat so I could understand how he worked. Joseph responded with an invitation to come to New Mexico for the re-opening of the Sound/Peace Chamber in Bernalillo, New Mexico, which had been closed for some time.

The revelation to build the chamber had come during a sacred Long Dance. Joseph had asked for a vision which would clarify how he could best contribute to the Earth and honor all alive and walking on its surface. He describes it this way:

> The Council of Elders came in a flash of light, a point of illumination which lasted about two or three seconds. The Council of Elders is that ever-unfolding moment fused with God's presence activating the livelihood of radiance of light from the Heavens and Earth. So I slowed down time and went back to have another look. I was shown people praying and singing together in sacred Sound Chambers resonating with light, the many colors of the rainbow. In the vision, the chamber was oval-shaped built half in and half out of the ground. As such it sits where the Earth and Sky meet, since one of its functions is to unite the masculine and feminine, the Sky and the Earth. In doing so, the chambers bring wholeness, harmony, and peace on an inner level to the individual, on a political level to all humanity, and on a cosmic level to the universe.

In the vision, Joseph was told to build ten Sound/Peace Chambers to be used for chanting in order to promote world peace. The word *sound* is part of the official title because, according to Joseph, *sound is the heart of God*. As of this writing there are some sixty chambers around the world.

Due to the unique nature of this trip, I wanted confirmation from Higher Mind before going to New Mexico. I telephoned seven people, both men and women, whom seemed to be the right persons to come to New Mexico for re-opening the chamber. They were in various parts of the United States, from Washington State to Washington, D.C. If all seven agreed to come, this would be a clear *yes*. If even one person did not accept, we would not go to New Mexico.

The universe was given a demanding assignment and responded quickly. At the appointed hour, each person called and agreed to come. It was yet another synchronous affirmation. Higher Mind was clearly in charge, orchestrating a convergence of people, places and events. Any lingering doubts were immediately dispelled and the trip to the Sound/Peace Chamber would proceed as planned.

As to the choice of the number *seven*, it was arbitrary—at least at the conscious level. I later learned seven is a significant number for Joseph. At 7pm on the seventh day of every month, he performs a special purification ceremony to help reconnect planetary consciousness with the spiritual realm of cosmic thought. He also invites others to light a candle at 7pm, wherever they are, and take a moment to pray for peace.

Upon landing at the airport on my first visit to Albuquerque, I immediately felt at home in this land of enchantment. The air is clean and easy to breathe, the landscape open and expansive with a peaceful palette of soft, muted desert colors. Joseph was waiting at the airport. Our first order of business was to rent a car, which just happened to be a red Sundance, an auspicious beginning since Joseph is a Sun Dancer. After meeting up with our group of seven, we drove to Bernalillo, a small town located about ten miles north of Albuquerque and arrived at the site of the Sound/Peace Chamber. We entered the chamber, a flat-roofed, elliptical adobe structure, with a sense of reverence.

When Joseph was given the vision to build the chamber, he started looking for some idyllic location, perhaps a scenic spot on a mountain or a secluded forested site somewhere. About a month after this, he was called before the same elders who had given him the vision to explain why he had not started building the chamber. He had no excuse to offer. An angel was sent to draw a circle of light on the ground next to the simple dwelling where he lived, a trailer with jerry-built additions. The search for the imagined perfect site was over. The next day, shovel in hand, he obediently began to dig the foundation for the chamber.

For years Joseph lived in that same humble dwelling next to the Sound/Peace Chamber with railroad tracks nearby. The sound of locomotive whistles and the rumbling vibration of the trains as they rolled rapidly down the steel tracks was ever-present. Rather than experiencing the trains as a disturbing nuisance, Joseph embraced the sounds from the trains as that which interrupts thoughts and keeps them from being crystallized. I was beginning to discover who Joseph is: *an innocent in love with life, one who lives from his heart and finds God's beauty in everything.*

Joseph tells the story of revisiting the beings on the other side that gave him the task of constructing sound/peace chambers and asking them why they had chosen him for this task. Somewhat tongue-in-cheek, he explains:

"Is it because I am bright?" I asked. "No" came the answer.

"Is it because I am talented?" "No" again.

"Because I am good-looking?" "No. None of these. You were given the task of building the chambers because you listen and do what you are told."

CHAPTER ONE

LISTENING IS GIVING

Training Ground of a Cosmic Dancer

JOSEPH WAS GIVEN THE TASK OF BUILDING THE SOUND/PEACE CHAMBERS because he knew *how to listen*. What training, experiences, or teachings had enhanced his ability to listen so deeply to the subtler levels of life? How was it possible for him to know from a thousand miles away when someone in his tribe makes their final transition from life, or listen silently to an unspoken question a person has waited a lifetime to resolve and give an answer recognized immediately as truth, or know information about the galaxies before it is published? All of this made me curious to find out about his background.

It is not by chance that Joseph comes from a Tiwa tradition which is deeply connected to the cosmos and Great Spirit. One of the first words Tiwa children learn is *no-con-who*, which means galaxy. These Native American descendants of the ancient Anasazi understand that everyone and everything is connected to the vastness of the galaxy and to the implicit order, the creative intelligence of the universe. Even the design of Picuris, the New Mexico pueblo where Joseph grew up, is carefully arranged to be in alignment with the sun, moon, stars, constellations, Pleiades, and so on, as though to gather the thoughts of the cosmos.

In such an environment, one feels those connections at a cellular level and is inspired to live in harmony and proper relationship with self, others, Mother Earth and universal order. He or she knows they are made of *appearing and disappearing light from the inhalation and exhalation of God's breath* and know that every mind is a vast universe made from the dust of innumerable stars. With that understanding, awareness is heightened and perception expands. It becomes easier to access numerous enlightened ideas that could be acted on in any single moment and explore any one of these insights and then shift, or dance, to the next idea and delve into that as well.

When someone is raised in that environment, at an early age he or she can move effortlessly into the inner planes and visit hundreds of other realities. Native born or not, people with these capacities are able to navigate in and out of other dimensions, other realities, and other landscapes. They go back in time to identify and heal a core issue. They see into the future. Their minds are focused, trained, ever present and aware. Their spiritual capacities are enhanced, and their hearts are open, compassionate, accepting and inclusive.

Such a person is a cosmic dancer, *an innocent who is danced by Higher Mind.* They are often engaged in a two-way communication with what quantum physicists call the implicate order, the creative intelligence of the universe. They are interdimensional beings committed to the highest insights and visions possible to guide earth's spiritual evolution forward for the good of all. They are the awakened species we are all in the process of becoming.

Enter Each Moment Fully

Even when a child shows an early disposition toward spiritual gifts, a certain amount of training is still necessary to refine their ability to listen and be attuned to the subtlest levels of vibration. Though it is not possible for an outsider to know all that was involved in Joseph's training, I can share what I heard, observed, and experienced firsthand. Each lesson, while demanding, offers a glimpse of the way one cosmic dancer learned to listen. And since we are all cosmic dancers in the making, we study these lessons and gather hints and inspirations which stir our own capacities.

From an early age, Joseph learned that in order to survive, he must adapt to many cultures, languages and environments. For someone destined to be a global figure, this was an important aspect of his training. As a child, he learned Spanish, English and Tiwa and quickly became proficient in all three languages.

He was shuffled from a bleak miner camp (where his father worked alongside African Americans and Chinese immigrants), to the Ute reservation (home of his mother's people where he heard mostly English and Spanish), and to Picuris Pueblo (home of his father's people) where Tiwa was spoken. In order to be accepted in different groups, he learned to listen carefully and adjust quickly so he could act appropriately in different cultures. Life required him to give full attention to whatever the moment asked.

From these experiences he learned *Listening is giving*: *To give is to enter each moment fully.* In virtually every piece of art Joseph creates, a profile of a face appears somewhere in the drawing. The eyes gaze as if to suggest we enter and travel through life *knowing.* The face is a metaphor of entering, or listening with full attention and giving oneself totally to *the holy moment.* It is a reminder that in any given moment we can either enter with awareness or choose to leave discounting or avoiding what the moment brings to our attention.

When the time came for Joseph to assume the global role of traveling and teaching worldwide, his early training served him well. He knew how to *listen* to how things were done in a home in a culture where he might be staying. When greeting another person, is it proper to bow, shake hands, nod, or kiss both cheeks? Do they remove their shoes at the door or keep them on? Are water glasses in the kitchen cabinets placed face down or face up? Most important, though, is when anyone, regardless of age, sex, race, culture, or tradition speaks with Joseph, he enters the moment with them and *listens,* or *gives,* with full attention.

The Key to Intuition

Learning to listen intuitively required another kind of training. When Joseph was only six, his mother died. Because his father was not able to care for all of the siblings, Joseph was placed in a foster home at Picuris soon after her death. Although he was a young boy, his foster parents expected him to do a man's work. His brothers thought his foster mother was harsh and demanded long and arduous hours of work. It was in this household where Joseph learned obedience, an old-fashioned term seldom used in today's world; it is the word Joseph uses to describe what he learned during this period of his life. No matter what was demanded, he listened respectfully and obeyed. He also realized if he didn't listen, he might be sent away—a sobering thought, since he had no other place to go.

Joseph says the key to intuition is to *listen to outer authority before one can listen to the inner voice of spirit. Once you can follow rules without questions, the shift from outer to inner authority becomes quite natural.* Thus, when you are told by Spirit to do something which may not make sense to the rational mind, you listen and do what you are told.

If we did not learn to be obedient to outer authority when we were young, we can still learn to follow our intuition. The process of listening within is similar to the way a mother learns to recognize her child's voice. The more she listens to that sound, the more she can identify it. If her child calls out to her on a crowded playground, she knows her child's voice even amid the voices of the other children.

Likewise, the more we listen to our intuitive or inner voice, the more certainty there is in distinguishing the sound of the true self from all the other voices that may be crying out to be heard—the voice of ego, or anger, or fear. And the more we listen to the inner voice, the more it speaks to us. Intuition comes in a variety of forms: a hunch, a feeling that persists, a revealing dream, a clear knowing, a sensing that defies the rational mind, and visceral responses (a warm sensation in the heart, a flash of light in the third eye, or energy rushing throughout the entire body).

The block to intuition for many of us is *doubt*. I recall an experience from my own childhood which illustrates this point well. Most of my childhood was spent in Front Royal, Virginia where sledding was a favorite winter outdoor activity. Along with the other neighborhood children, we often sledded down a carefully marked, meandering path on what was called the Van Duesen Hill. On one particular afternoon with Joanna and John, my two older siblings, we decided to sled down our driveway. It opened onto Virginia Avenue which was a wide, quiet street lined with large elm trees.

Everything went well until dad arrived home early. Seeing the obvious danger in the way we were sledding, he immediately summoned us inside and asked each of us the same question:

"What would you do, if when you got to the end of the driveway, a car came down the street?" Joanna's answer was, "get real flat." To which dad quipped, "You don't have to worry about that. The car would make you flat enough."

John was questioned next and confidently said he would "quickly roll off the sled." Then came my turn. I knew the answer. It was obvious—roll off the sled. But here is where *doubt* entered. John had already given this answer. Repeating what John said would seem like copying. In that moment my mind, or doubt, got in the way and intuition was forgotten. My rational mind was trying to be safe and be *politically correct*. My response was a weak, "I don't know." Needless to say, that was the end of our driveway sledding. The next day we went back to sledding on the Van Deusen Hill which did not empty into a street.

The *I Ching,* the Chinese book of Changes, explains the process of understanding intuition this way. When Heaven and Earth come together, they give birth to the *first son*, our first thought—intuition. On the heels of the first son, the *second son*, doubt, the rational mind is born. The second son appears in any number of ways: when wanting to please others, when influenced by the unspoken but powerful influence of consensus reality, or when we second-guess our choices.

Whenever or however doubt is born, we must then *go to the high mountain*, the place of inner stillness and give birth to the *third son,* clear knowing. We might delay an important decision until we have had time to quiet ourselves and listen to our deepest truth. I observed that Joseph did not focus on doubt. Thus, he is apprised of clear knowing.

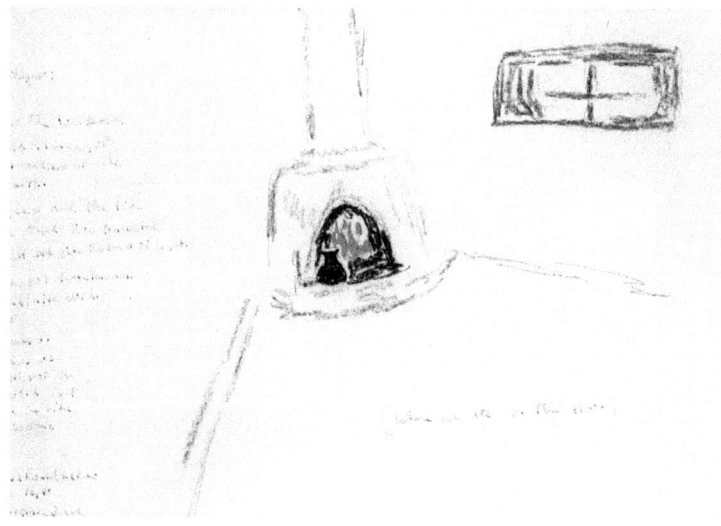

Pay Attention

On a different note, Joseph spent a year living with his beloved grandmother at Picuris Pueblo. Here he had an opportunity to learn the art of listening in a significantly different way. This very wise woman taught him to *pay attention,* to see the extraordinary in the ordinary and discern the difference between appearance and true reality.

Joseph fondly remembers his grandmother sweeping the dirt floor of her two- room house with a hand brush made of sage from the fields. As she performed her daily tasks, he was learning all the while the deeper meaning of beauty. The brush she swept with was *holy* because the herb from which it was fashioned was considered sacred. Thus, sweeping the floor and cleaning the house was really a ceremony of beautification which opened the gateway to awareness. Joseph saw that all tasks done with *mindfulness* were ceremonies in daily life and work is actually a form of worship.

As she vigorously swept the floors, she created a small dust storm in which she would periodically disappear. Then from the dust he would see the familiar small, plump figure emerge once more. When she was sweeping, he and the other children would all try to keep out of her way, for nothing was safe in her path. Dust, she would say, was the essence of transcendence. She would remind them to *pay attention* so they would not miss the voices of their ancestors who were there to help them be good people.

Subtle Listening

Perhaps the pivotal teacher in Joseph's training in learning to listen was his grandfather, a medicine man with whom he spent a great deal of time. Once, Joseph saw his grandfather effortlessly go through a wall in the kiva, the underground chamber where ceremonies and teachings are taught to males. He returned with a flower and reminded Joseph that walking through walls would not be a part of his medicine, for he would have other gifts.

On another occasion, a particular night with his grandfather remains vividly in Joseph's memory. It went something like this: *You have been with me many times in the underground kiva. Tonight, we are going down the stepladder and spend the night in the kiva. He then lit a fire. The flickering light of the fire, the shadows etched on the walls and the crackling sound of burning logs added a sense of anticipation and mystery to the evening. Lie down and we will sleep back to back throughout the night. Joseph did exactly as he was told. He soon began to feel electrical charges of energy sent from his grandfather which pulsed throughout his entire body.*

According to Joseph, the back is a metaphor of the past. Thus, that night the ancient teachings were passed on from grandfather to grandson. How beautiful! The story of that particular evening leaves us somewhat speechless.

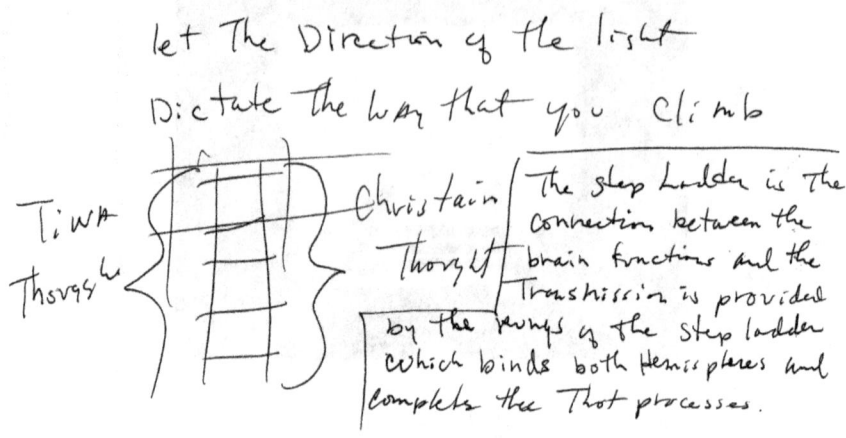

Through the Eyes of an Innocent

The importance of memory and the connection between listening and memory were ever present to Joseph. As is true of most Native people, Joseph comes from an oral tradition where one learns to listen and retain what one hears. There was a time when Joseph asked his students **not** to take notes when he was teaching. He soon realized how difficult it is for most people not to write down what they hear as an aid to memory. It was just too great an imprint to overcome. After a while, he stopped making that request.

Note-taking did not exist in Joseph's training ground, for it was considered a left brain activity, a function of the rational mind. Instead, listening was emphasized because *true listening* enhances memory. *God is breath, matter and movement,* and memory is *vibration retained in matter.*

The importance of memory was once again brought home when we attended a talk at the North Carolina Sound/Peace Chamber. The speaker was a visiting Maori chief from New Zealand who was accompanied by his apprentice. His student was learning to memorize and then recite perfectly the entire genealogy of his people which, we were told, takes about six hours. If he were to make a mistake at any point, he must begin all over again. It is a stringent discipline. The rewards of this practice, however, are an impeccably well-trained mind and an unimpeachable memory.

When one fully *enters the moment, and looks through the eyes of an innocent child, the memories of all things become available.* As with Joseph and the Maori student as well as most indigenous peoples (especially those from cultures with no written language) memory is valued. It is thought to be essential.

The memory training this young Maori is receiving will allow him to *remember,* or listen inwardly to useful information for individuals in his tribe, or for the tribe or perhaps even the entire world. When truly innocent, we *remember* what is needed. No trance or special technique is required. A favorite passage from the New Testament (John 14:26) comes to mind, "I will bring forth to thy remembrance whatsoever you have need of from the foundations of the earth."

It is only when we are *without thought* that we are given exactly what is needed. An artist starts a painting trusting the process of not knowing exactly what will unfold. A chef begins with a time-worn recipe and makes changes because he is guided to do something quite different. A grandmother senses exactly what is needed to soothe the feelings of her hurt grandchild. Or a caring stranger may spontaneously say the very thing needed for a distressed fellow passenger on an airplane. Pause a moment and reflect on when you are able to *look* through the eyes of an innocent child, those moments when you are present, totally alive, in the eternal now.

Develop the Capacity of Sensitivity

No training in listening would be complete without developing the capacity of sensitivity. This faculty can be cultivated in several ways. For Joseph, the path to sensitivity was through sound. To understand all physical forms as sound and vibrations of the infinite Self and to be a working listener to those forms became the focus of his life.

Because Joseph did not read until he was twelve, his school teachers assumed he was just another "dumb Indian." Joseph would often skip school and spend his days in the mountains where Mother Earth was his teacher. There he acquired sensitivity to the deeper mysteries of sound and vibration. In *Being and Vibration,* the book we co-authored, the subject of sound is explored in depth.

At age twelve, Joseph's experience with school improved dramatically. He realized if he psychically brought the blackboard closer to him, he could read what was written on it. The problem was not due to lack of intelligence but to weak eyes. Thereafter, he excelled in school and eventually earned a master's degree in political science from the University of Wisconsin.

Listening to Nature

Joseph learned to listen deeply in nature, to perceive the ephemeral sound and vibration of a bird flying overhead, or a leaf falling, or a puma approaching from a distance, or the subtle changes in weather. At one point, Joseph was told by his medicine teachers to go find a certain herb, a plant that did not grow near the pueblo but could only be found some twenty miles or so up in the mountains. He was given the name and description of the plant and told not to return home until he found it. When he asked how he could locate it, the response was to call out to the plant and listen for it to respond to him. Some days later, Joseph returned with the herb.

When one develops the capacity of sensitivity, we hear Great Mystery speaking through everything. For when we are listening, God is also listening. The letter L, the first letter of the word *listening*, is a symbol for God in several cultures, so *when we listen we are in the company of God.* It becomes possible to know the healing sound needed for each organ of the body, sense the untold story beneath the one that is told, hear a cry for help from a thousand miles away, know of things to come, hear the collective non-verbal sound of a group, and know how to enter silence.

CHAPTER TWO

METAPHORS ARE THE LANGUAGE OF UNIVERSAL CONSCIOUSNESS

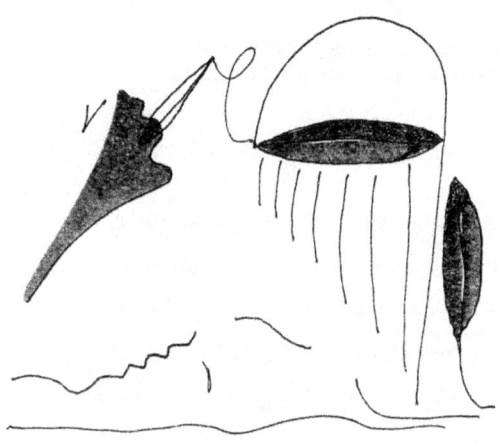

Awakened Awareness

THE FACTS OF 9/11 ARE FAMILIAR TO ALL. Alongside these facts, another story was being told. Almost immediately Joseph observed that the animals on the land where he lives came out of their dens and hiding places. They felt the unmistakable shift in the collective vibration from fear to love. Suddenly it was safe to be more vulnerable and trusting. The vulnerability and openness of the animals was a metaphor linked to the vulnerability and openness we all felt on that day.

Metaphorically, it could be said those who were sacrificed that day awakened us to love. As a people, we became united for one moment in time and remembered the oneness of humankind. We were One People. One Earth. We realized what happens to one impacts all.

Reality is pregnant with hidden meanings. What we believe and think is only one part of true reality and by itself may lead us away from truth. When we use this understanding of reality alongside metaphor, which is *awakened awareness*, we join body to soul.

Metaphors are not understood with the mind in the usual sense. They evoke direct personal responses which are deep, nonverbal, visceral and transformative. What we experience occurs within us and to different parts of our physical bodies which then connects us to new insights and perceptions.

Metaphors exist in every culture and every tradition. They can be found in literature, art, music, dance, nature, ceremonies and celebrations, in nighttime dreams and in the waking dream of everyday life. In whatever form they appear, *metaphors are the language of universal consciousness and transport us to the more expansive perception of Higher Mind.*

All Life is Metaphor in the Mind of God

The first time Joseph and I taught together, we were scheduled for a series of three programs back to back in New Mexico. My son John, then a student at the University of Virginia, was slated to fly out to Albuquerque and drive one of the vans transporting participants to and from various sites.

Upon arrival in New Mexico, I immediately let Joseph know that John was ill with a high fever and stomach virus and would not be coming. We gathered at the Sound/Peace Chamber in Bernalillo as soon as everyone arrived. In his typical understated manner, Joseph announced we were going to perform a healing for John. He asked everyone to close their eyes and focus on a jackrabbit. A *jackrabbit?* For most of us, this was foreign to our ears. We learned later that the jackrabbit is a metaphor for healing.

As requested, everyone in the chamber closed their eyes and focused on the rabbit. Joseph asked each person what they experienced. Almost everyone described feeling a cool breeze (a metaphor for Spirit) and the sudden shift in temperature circling the interior of the chamber. Some saw images. I saw John's head with a headband hovering in the sky above a pueblo which later proved to be Picuris. The significance of the headband went ignored. It was only later when I noticed that Joseph wears a headband when he does prayers and ceremonies to bring attention to Higher Mind.

Do I often see images of people "hovering overhead"? Not at all. Keep in mind we were in a sacred Sound/Peace Chamber where perception is heightened. In many ways this episode was a major threshold crossing. We entered the metaphoric world at a much more profound level. It is a world

METAPHORS ARE THE LANGUAGE OF UNIVERSAL CONSCIOUSNESS

nuanced with images, mystery, and insights that leave us breathless and allow us to fall totally and completely in love with life.

After the ceremony, we boarded our vans and left for Picuris for the annual August 10th Feast Day celebrations. When we were about twenty miles from the pueblo, Joseph had the drivers pull over to a road stop so we could get out of our vehicles and view the magnificence of the Rio Grande and the Sangre de Cristo Range.

Then, unexpectedly, Joseph said we were going to do another ceremony for John. He proceeded to open a loaf of bread and began to tear off small pieces, placing them randomly on an ant hill. (When no one was watching, he moved catlike. Without drawing any attention to himself, he placed bread on two other hills repeating the same ritual.) No explanation was given as to the purpose of the bread. With the ceremony apparently complete, we returned to our vans and drove the remaining miles to Picuris where we enjoyed a full day of feasting, dances and ceremonies.

On the way back from Picuris, we stopped at the same spot on the side of the road. Joseph very matter-of-factly said, "We are going to see how John is doing." By now it was dark, so Joseph grabbed his flashlight and headed toward the first ant hill. He quickly surveyed the mound. No bread and no ants. He made a sound, a deep "mmm", but said nothing. He then went to the second hill, then the third. There was no bread and no ants. Then with a final, "mmm, wow," Joseph turned and said, "Tell John the entire ant kingdom is participating in his healing." It was a perplexing statement.

I reminded myself that remarks were intended for John, not for me. My role was simply to be the messenger. Early the next morning I phoned John, "How are you feeling?" His answer was, "A lot better. In fact, I feel cool. I've had a quick turn-around."

As to Joseph's message? John's reply was direct, "Tell Joseph, thank you. I understand. To the Native American, all life is metaphor in the mind of God."

Synchronistic at its best! John had just received high marks in a course on Carlos Castaneda at the University of Virginia. Though Joseph had only met John briefly five years earlier at the medicine wheel seminar, he sensed he was no newcomer to the world of metaphor and the seemingly miraculous. John caught the next available flight and joined us in New Mexico.

PS. This ceremony was a real stretch for me and the group. Keep in mind it was spontaneously created for John and only John. Probably, this ceremony will never be repeated. It was a response to a particular person and his need. John fully understood the metaphors in this ceremony and was healed in the process.

Understanding Metaphors

We asked for more instruction. We needed Joseph to explain the deeper meaning of John's ceremony and the pole-climbing ceremony which we had all observed at Picuris.

We had seen the Koshare (medicine men painted in black and white, a metaphor for duality and the paradoxes of life) playfully attempt to climb a pole which was placed in the center of the pueblo. The pole is a tree which is stripped of its bark and towers some forty feet in the air. Secured with rope at the top of the pole is a freshly-killed sheep (representing the foundation of life), bread (beautiful light), and a watermelon (light that has been ripened). After several failed attempts at climbing the pole, only one Koshare makes a successful ascent. He then unties the ropes and lowers the bounty back to Earth.

This pole-climbing ceremony might be observed many times without understanding what the ceremony is teaching. The Koshare shimmy up the pole in ant-like fashion. In metaphor, they climb to the higher worlds where everything is possible and return with *insights* for the *people* (the collective vibration).

Joseph explained that the ant world and the Higher Worlds are inextricably interconnected. So when he was feeding the ants by the side of the road on our way to Picuris, he was purposefully enlisting Higher Mind to assist in healing John. While the ants were eating the bread, simultaneously the Koshare were bringing down bread (Light) which heals and clarifies.

This story is included not only because it is a true story which occurred while walking with a cosmic dancer but is an example of metaphor at its subtlest level. When we are learning something new, whether it is in art, music, sports, or business, we are eager to learn from those who have refined their gifts and skills.

Thus, we learn the language of metaphors from those who have mastered this universal language.

METAPHORS ARE THE LANGUAGE OF UNIVERSAL CONSCIOUSNESS

    The teachings of Carl Jung, renowned Swiss psychotherapist, are filled with the wisdom of archetypes and metaphors and are a good place to learn about metaphors in particular. According to some of the locals of Picuris, one person who frequented their feast days was none other than Carl Jung himself. The locals referred to him as the man with the 'crazy green hat' or was it the 'crazy man with the green hat.' Green hat aside, he enjoyed coming to the festivities and ceremonial dances at Picuris.

    Like many others, not only was he enjoying the exquisite beauty of the dancers and the antics of the Koshare, but also was both reading and relishing the archetypes and metaphors being enacted at a deeply profound level.

The Village Ceremonial Pole that brings in the Living light so that The People may Live.

28

17

One Form Leads to Another

There are several ways a person learns to understand metaphors. Sometimes we *walk with a question* on the lips of our mind before the veracity of a metaphor is revealed and truth resonates through body and soul.

Still another way to understand metaphors is to create a direct, personal experience with whatever it is you want to explore. We replace the mental level of borrowed, second-hand experience with the metaphoric level, where imagination and heart are nourished.

Joseph once demonstrated this by explaining how prayer ties are used in ceremonies and each bundle carries a prayer. *You might become curious and want to discover more, so you decide to make fifty prayer ties. You begin by cutting small cloth squares and placing tobacco in each square, then carefully tie each bundle with string. In doing this, you are not only working with cloth and string but are also working with your fingers.*

In the metaphoric world, *one form carries another form* and then to another, like a chain reaction, similar to how the mind works. We start reflecting on what the metaphor of something might be and soon we have an insight which then takes us to another insight. We begin to sense that fingers are a very ancient moving form which awakens gifts that come from the spiritual realm. We discover that not only are you making prayer ties, but as you work with your fingers, you are sowing seeds which will manifest in your life.

Once the prayer ties are made, you can use them for an upcoming ceremonial dance and place them lovingly on a tree at the dance site knowing those prayers will be there for one year. In the process, prayer ties, once an unquantified entity, have become a deeply personal, life-giving image.

Metaphors and Sensitivity

On more than one occasion, Joseph taught our groups how to see tree spirits. He would ask everyone to sit or lie down outside just when it was beginning to get dark. This is the easiest time to see the energy around trees. He instructed everyone to find a comfortable spot, relax, keep focused on the trees, and then let your eyes go slowly out of focus. Soon you will begin to see what lies slightly *beyond* the trees. If you can see the tree spirits, you might later begin to see the cloud beings or the rock beings or the corn beings, because every natural kingdom has spirits which watch over it. That knowledge, so basic to indigenous people who have never forgotten the language of the land, is often new to those of us over-burdened by civilization.

Seeing the spirit of the tree is one way of recognizing that all life is an expression of the Divine. Every living thing and even every inanimate object carries an indwelling spirit. When we sense the aliveness of the universe, whether we see nature spirits or not, we have reverence for all life.

Joseph reminds us to give something back when we cut a plant or take something from nature. It could be a strand of hair or an offering of corn meal or a pinch of tobacco. I also know he has never intentionally killed an animal or insect of any kind. Of course, Joseph lives in a time when hunting is no longer a necessity for most people. It is also important to remember his ancestors always hunted with reverence for their quarry.

It is probably because of his reverence for life that he can communicate with different species. At one point, ants began to invade the Sound/Peace Chamber. When he asked them to leave, they did. And, when people go on vision quests with Joseph, they are comforted in knowing that they will not be bothered by snakes or other uninvited guests.

If we can see the spirit of a tree, it also means we see the spirit in all life. An experience I witnessed in Holland comes to mind. While gazing out a solarium window, I noticed a grandfather and his grandchild spending time together enjoying the beauty of their garden. Suddenly, Mara discovered a dead bird. She immediately got a trowel and began to bury the bird in a special spot in the garden and even made a garland of flowers which she placed ever so delicately on the burial site. Next, she spontaneously burst into song celebrating the life of this special bird. Because she is so connected with the spirit inside her own being, she was able to feel the spirit of the bird.

When we truly know *everything* is alive, we want to know its Spirit story. The Spirit story each living thing carries is conveyed in the language of the soul, which is metaphor. Rocks are just rocks until we realize they carry the mother energy; a tree is just a tree until we know it reminds us of our greatness; and kneeling is just kneeling until we know that when we kneel we bring something to completion.

Stay Open to the Moment

Metaphors can surprise us. We never know what metaphor might show up and are reminded to stay open to the moment, knowing that whatever presents itself is exactly what is needed. A case in point was a Long Dance I led in northern Louisiana some years ago. Through visionary experience, Joseph has created three dances: The *Long Dance* (to bring into existence what we seek), the *Drum Dance* (to be able to see what kinds of seeds we are planting for the future generations), and the *Sun/Moon Dance* (to be able to see the active-passive existence of life inside perceptual reality).

A Long Dance is an overnight ceremonial dance which begins at twilight and ends at daybreak. In preparation for the ceremony, each dancer paints or draws a personal medicine shield, a metaphoric representation of the intent of his or her dance. The participants then stake these shields around the dance site. Once the Long Dance begins, dancers dance and drummers drum and chant during the entire nocturnal ceremony.

The site for our dance was a bucolic idyll: rolling, lush green pastures underfoot and a star-studded sky overhead. Just as we were beginning our dance, coyotes nearby began to howl. Traditionally, coyotes symbolize the *trickster* element. They bring the unexpected—shocks, surprises, abrupt shifts—and make us question our perception of reality. It wasn't long into the dance before the trickster made itself known. The wind unexpectedly blew a foul stench right into the middle of our dance site. It was the unmistakable smell of death.

It is common practice in farm life to leave a dead animal over by a fence where it eventually decomposes or is consumed by wild animals and carrion fowl. Throughout the dance, the smell would disappear and then unexpectedly reappear. Some of us wanted to throw up! This was not the atmosphere we were expecting for our spiritual experience! But as we continued to focus on the beat of the drums and the rhythms of nature around us, we became less distracted by our five physical senses and open to a more profound awareness. We were reminded that life and death go together side by side. In those moments, we transcended judgment of life and death, good and bad, right and wrong, light and dark and accepted what is.

When the long-awaited light of morning arrived and the drummers finished their last chant, a chorus of birds burst forth with melodious song . . . perhaps the song of the birds was affirming our shift in perception.

I was reminded of the Koshare clowns at the Picuris Pueblo Feast Day.

Painted in horizontal bands of black and white, they represent the duality of paradox. They challenge the crowd with antics and surprises and jolt us out of our limited either/or thinking.

What we think we know is not what is. The Koshare clowns remind us to transcend the apparent duality of life. The life/death paradox is only one of many seemingly contradictory energies we may confront. We shut down or we explode; we are co-dependent or anti-dependent; we are generous to a fault or don't give enough.

Whenever there is paradox, we are reminded in metaphor to climb the pole to Higher Consciousness. In that space we hold the opposites, accepting everything, including the paradoxes of life, as a part of the awesome mystery.

Metaphors in Our Daily Lives

It is important to become aware of the metaphors being played out in our everyday life. Since *metaphors are the language of Higher Consciousness,* Joseph would often ask: "What is the metaphor? What is Higher Mind communicating?"

Even small things can be great teachers. What is the metaphor of repeatedly locking yourself out of your car? It may be you are not connected to your body. Not grounded. What is the metaphor of where you have clutter? Maybe at work, your office is meticulous. In the outer world, you are clear and responsible. Your bedroom, on the other hand, is untidy, a metaphor of how you treat yourself in your private space. What is the metaphor of 'forgetting' to return a book to someone? Is letting things slide an overall pattern that repeats or is there some unresolved issue with the person whose book you borrowed? What about not using a gift certificate from a store you like? Do you unconsciously avoid the abundance you could have in this and other areas of your life?

Quantum physics reminds us that we are essentially holograms. One aspect of ourselves reflects and impacts the whole of our life. Thus, little changes in our lives are mirrored everywhere. As we make seemingly minor changes, we experience a corresponding shift in our outer world. Clearing the clutter helps free the mind of attachment to the past and forms that no longer serve, returning a book promptly indicates we are able to deal with things as they present themselves, and using a gift certificate before it expires affirms our self-worth and our willingness to receive abundance in other areas of our life.

We are inspired to decode the language of metaphors in our everyday life and embrace the awareness that *all life is metaphor in the mind of God.*

CHAPTER THREE

ALL CEREMONIES REFLECT THE DESIRE TO GET IN TOUCH WITH HIGHER MIND

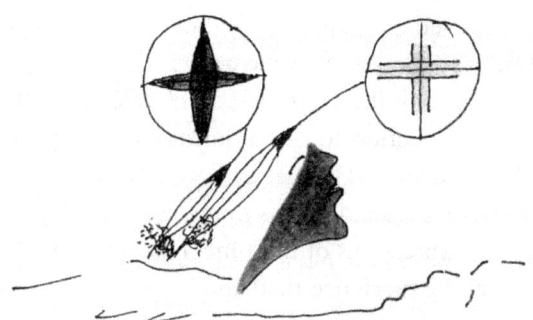

Mysteries of Ceremony

Ceremony is a universal form of expression. *All ceremonies, whether they be ancient forms passed from one generation to another or ceremonies created in the spontaneity of the moment, are the result of the desire to get in touch with Higher Mind.* When we lose sight of the beauty of existence, we get out of tune. Ceremonies lead us back into beauty and anchor us solidly in a sacred space where we feel our spirit and remember who we are.

The foundation for all ceremony is beauty and the radiance of light that allows us to see with childlike innocence. In those moments, we connect the Earth to Heaven and bring Heaven to Earth. We send blessings not just for the here and now, but for the future as well.

The ancients knew ceremonies give energy to those who are involved. Everyone receives a blessing, not just the physical beings on this plane but those on the inner planes and in all other realities as well. We send light from the center of the ceremony to the four directions, east, south, west and north, representing the mental, emotional, physical and spiritual aspects of our being.

It is a good ceremony when we sense Divine Presence. This state of grace may last only a matter of seconds. Nevertheless, it is long enough to know with certainty that we have indeed touched the timeless realm.

Falling in Love with Ceremony

As a child raised in the Baptist tradition, my experience with ceremony was limited. There was a brief exposure to weddings, funerals and baptism where one was immersed in water as a symbol of being born into a new life. There was also the Baptist-style communion service which I remember more because of the grape juice and stale bread than anything else. However, my introduction to ceremonies at a more profound level, happened quite by chance.

Even as a very young child, I always knew there is only one truth, one spirit, and many expressions of the One. That awareness created a longing to explore and experience firsthand some of the ways unifying truth is expressed. I wanted to appreciate the many different facets of the one beautiful diamond. It was a soulful stirring call that would become a lifelong quest.

By the age of seven, I had read about the Islamic tradition and was impressed with their call to prayer five times a day. Since Front Royal did not have a mosque and I didn't know any Muslim prayers, the Baptist prayers had to do. It was summer which meant interrupt outdoor activities, go to my bedroom, kneel, facing east and pray. It did not take long before the five-times-a-day prayer ritual interfered with play and play was extremely important. Thus, my experiment with Islam was of short duration.

My next plan was to visit the various churches in town. I decided to go as usual to Sunday school at the Baptist church where my family and I were members. Then, instead of attending the eleven o'clock service at First Baptist, I would visit other churches. Since my father attended the Baptist Men's Bible class and not the church service and my mother directed the choir at the Presbyterian Church, no one would be the wiser. This was to be a solo experiment. I really didn't think anyone my age would find this interesting! I also decided not to tell my parents the plan knowing they would veto the idea.

First was the Lutheran church, followed by the Methodist, then the Episcopal. All of the churches were within several blocks of each other, so walking to any of them was easy. Each was interesting, but no church warranted a second visit. Next was the Catholic Church.

As soon as I opened the door and entered the sanctuary, I felt enveloped in what can only be described as *holiness*. There were kneeling benches, Latin liturgy, holy water, genuflections, chants, statues, rosaries, gestures and words which took on a greater meaning than I could grasp. The ritual and ceremony were all new and beautiful to my Baptist eyes. I was filled with awe and wonder. "Now this is a real service," I thought with great satisfaction. Finally, I had found my church.

I began to attend mass regularly. Since this was a covert operation, I wanted to be unnoticed, invisible, so quickly found a way to blend in anonymously with the congregation. I would cross myself, genuflect and quickly scan the congregation and look for the blonde people. So if I sat on a pew with blonde hair like mine, no would notice. The plan worked— that is, until one memorable Midsummer Day.

On that particular Sunday, it was unusually hot and humid and the church was not air-conditioned. The priest lit the incense and began to chant in a melodious, rhythmic fashion, swinging the gold censer back and forth, again and again. This ritual, I discovered later, is a ceremony performed as part of the Benediction service, a blessing given at the closing of Mass. But, on this sultry July day and sitting near the front of the church, the heavy pungent smoke of the incense soon became overwhelming. As my eyes moved back and forth following the pendulous movement of the censer, the voice of the priest became ever so faint. Things around me began to blur; red and gold and white merged together. I became extremely weak. All of a sudden, I passed out.

I don't know how long I was unconscious, nor do I know whether the priest finished the service or stopped abruptly when I keeled over. I remember only visiting a timeless place of pure peace. It was not an experience that was pursued, but one stumbled onto. As Joseph Campbell reminds us, where we stumble is where we inadvertently find our treasure.

A story from the *Arabian Nights* speaks of a farmer who is working in the fields when his plow gets stuck in a ring of some sort. He is vexed, but when he pulls on the ring, he discovers a cave filled with jewels. Metaphorically speaking, our psyche is a cave of jewels. When we allow ourselves to fully enter an experience, even if it is not what we were expecting, we discover deeper parts of ourselves. As it was with the farmer, so it was for me. An expected *stumbling* would prove to be a gift of great importance.

When I awoke in the church, I was lying on my back on the mahogany pew with a cold cloth on my forehead. Peering over me were the concerned faces of the priest and some parishioners who had gathered round to offer their assistance.

There was silence . . . Then, the priest spoke: "Whose child is this?" Of course, no one came forth to claim me. It felt strange to be nameless and not belong. There was a long, awkward pause. Finally, I felt compelled to speak. I said simply, "I'm Betty Marlow and I'm here by myself."

The priest was taken aback and for a moment didn't seem to know what to do. He then asked a good Catholic family if they would return me safely home. My new family helped me up and kindly took me to their car. When we pulled up in front of my house, my father happened to be sitting on the front porch reading the Sunday paper. How shocked he was to see his seven-year-old daughter emerge from an unfamiliar car driven by strangers—and Catholics at that! I waved a pleasant goodbye and walked up on the porch where daddy sat waiting. Needless to say, I had some explaining to do.

That was the end of my Roman Catholic experience, at least for the moment. However, it was just the beginning of my catholic (meaning *universal*) experience. In moments of purity and innocence we stumble and discover inclinations and longings that are part of God's "thumbprint" on our soul. A catalyst (in this case, the ceremony which took me immediately to the transcendent realm) may give us just a whiff or hint of something that will later be reintroduced. The full initiation into a new aspect of ourselves is often gradual, taking months or even years to unfold.

Powerful experiences such as this one often fade in importance or are forgotten for a while because we do not yet have a vessel strong enough or deep enough to hold such evanescent ecstasy. On that Sunday morning in a small Catholic church, something stirred in my soul, for I had unexpectedly fallen in love with ceremony, a heart song that could not be dismissed or overlooked. Such innate, deep-seated impulses cannot lie dormant forever. Years later at the right moment and time, and with Joseph serving as catalyst, ceremonies found their way back into my life.

ALL CEREMONIES REFLECT THE DESIRE TO GET IN TOUCH WITH HIGHER MIND

Ancient Ceremony

When Joseph and I taught together, we included both spontaneous ceremonies and ancient traditional ceremonies, like the Native American Sweat lodge (a purification ceremony) and the Vision Quest (a ceremony to experience visions and discover one's path). Whatever the ceremony, Joseph always silently asks permission from Great Spirit before he proceeds.

A particular Vision Quest comes to mind in which Deborah, one of the participants, had a most memorable experience. When the group gathered, Joseph let everyone know he was going to place each person in a spot on the mountain in such a way that they could not see the others. She remembers Joseph using these words as he talked to the group: "After you've been sitting in the sun for a while, you will probably get hot or tired. You'll be really angry at me before it's over, wondering what the heck am I doing here? You'll think, I'm hot, I'm sweaty. My back hurts. I'm crazy for even being here."

Meanwhile, Deborah was thinking: '*Well, that certainly won't be me*'. Joseph continued, "When you get angry, really angry, when you get to that point, stop—close your eyes, breathe, go into the experience—because that is when something crucial can happen."

"How long will we be in our spot?" Deborah wanted to know. "I don't know, I just work here. When you hear the sound of the drum, come back to the Sound/Peace Chamber."

Deborah was placed along with the others in her spot on the mountain. She sat there quietly meditating, when suddenly she heard something unusual. At first she thought it might be an animal. To calm herself she began to meditate once more. Then again . . . a sound like something breathing. *I am scared. My heart is pounding. Could it be a bear? I don't see anything.* She closed her eyes. *Am I imagining something? No, I hear it again. I hear two breaths; heavy breathing . . . one that is not mine . . . I know what it is . . . it is the Earth breathing.*

When the drum began to beat after several days, the participants on the vision quest left their assigned places and gathered together in the chamber. Those who wished to share experiences and insights from their vision quests did so. Deborah was still in shock. Finally, she gathered courage enough to tell her story. Joseph smiled and said, "You are absolutely right. That *is* the Earth breathing. Pay attention, *because the Earth will give you your name.* "We don't just have one name. A name depends on the phase of your life. When the Earth gives you your name, keep it a secret. Don't tell anybody."

About three months later while she was meditating with a group outdoors in Colorado, the Earth gave her another name. That one, though, is a secret she carries in her heart.

Spontaneous Ceremonies

Ninety percent of the ceremonies that Joseph conducts are spontaneous. They arise from being in tune with the moment. When sharing with Joseph that I was having writer's block, he created a brief ceremony to remedy the situation. He draped an elk's hide over a chair and asked me to sit in the chair. The elk is a metaphor for writing so the very act of sitting on an elk's hide placed me in direct contact with writing energy.

As is so often the case with ceremony, the concrete metaphor (in this case the elk hide) becomes the agent of transformation. Almost immediately, I felt a pain in the back of my neck. It was a message that something from the past was hindering my writing. Joseph took up his eagle feather. With a brush of the feather, the block was removed. The inspiration to write returned shortly thereafter.

Another experience comes to mind which again illustrates a ceremony born of the present moment. Joseph and I were conversing about the paradoxical nature of life. I was sharing a personal story of being simultaneously both ahead in some areas and behind in others, a contradiction set up in childhood. He responded with a simple yet potent spontaneous ceremony to help get me back *in time*.

As I sat in a chair, Joseph blew four breaths over the top of my head, one to each of the four directions: the mental, emotional, physical and spiritual. Since God is breath, matter and movement, the breath took me back to where I needed to be to regain equilibrium. In returning to the source of the issue, we can expedite the healing process.

Ceremony to Welcome the Night

Whenever Joseph and I taught together, we had a plan—and there was no plan. Whatever the moment asked of us always took precedence over any preconceived ideas. In Chaco Canyon, an important site of Anasazi

ALL CEREMONIES REFLECT THE DESIRE TO GET IN TOUCH WITH HIGHER MIND

Chaco Canyon

culture where an ancient people lived in harmony with the land, Joseph spontaneously created a memorable ceremony to welcome the night. As dusk approached, we headed with our group to an isolated part of the canyon, arriving just as the light was fading and night was falling. In many traditions twilight is considered an auspicious time. It is when the veil between the worlds is very thin.

The ground in this particular area of the canyon is composed mostly of hardpan, created by the unrelenting rays of the sun beating down upon it day after day. We walked in hushed silence which amplified the eerie crunch of our footfalls on earth where the ancient ones once walked. We knew we were privileged to enter this pristine, primordial corner of a most sacred site. When we stopped near a precipice overlooking the canyon, Joseph asked everyone to come to the edge so we could enjoy a more expansive view of Chaco.

Almost immediately, we began to celebrate the magnificence of the moment in a spontaneous ceremony. Amid the backdrop of a vast sky growing dark with the onset of night, Joseph started to chant ancient melodious sounds in Tiwa. In response, we danced in place. We danced first to the setting sun, turned, then danced in place facing the stars emerging in the East. And we danced to welcome the night, the place where we search for that which calls us. This cyclical back-and-forth dance continued until the sun bowed its head and its light faded quietly from the western horizon. It was ceremony at its best, a timeless moment filled with beauty and grace.

Ceremony to Release the Past

Soon after meeting Joseph, I asked him if there is a ceremony which could help me resolve a pattern I just couldn't seem to overcome. He was quick to respond, "Take a clay pot in your hands, raise your arms up high in front of you and state what you are letting go of. Then drop the pot on a rock so it breaks." On Easter morning (traditionally the time of rebirth) I walked along the Virginia Beach oceanfront carrying a carefully selected and rather primitively conceived clay pot. It was one of my friend's first 'practice' pots. She had been proud of the vessel at the time of its creation, but had since moved on to better work. It seemed the perfect metaphor to represent an old pattern which no longer served.

I went to an isolated area of the beach and located a suitably substantial rock. Holding the pot up high with my arms outstretched and naming out loud my intention for the ceremony, the pot was dropped directly on the rock. The vessel shattered completely. Simultaneously, I heard the mellifluous *music of the spheres* surrounding me and filling every part of my being.

Hearing celestial music is not uncommon, for many have heard music from other realms in specific circumstances. There are numerous references to *stars singing* as well as the music of the spheres in the readings of Edgar Cayce. Astronomer, alchemist and mystic Johannes Kepler, known for his formulation of the laws of planetary motion, not only saw harmony in the movements of the planets but spoke often of hearing the music of the spheres as well.

James Mullaney, director of the DuPont Planetarium, informs us that the Sun and all of the stars and the galaxies they make up, including our Milky Way, emit radiation across the entire electromagnetic spectrum. This includes not only ultraviolet, infrared and visible light, but radio waves as well—emissions which can be converted to audible sounds. Thanks to giant telescopes, powerful supercomputers and sophisticated electronic synthesizers, radio astronomers have discovered harmonic vibrations (not random noise) coming from a number of the stars.

Thus, in a sense stars are *singing* to us. As Mullaney says, this new technology makes it possible to "listen to the cosmos with our ears as well as look at it with our eyes". These sounds from the universe, now a proven fact, have always been of importance to the subtle ears of mystics.

I told Joseph about my ceremony, the release in letting go, and my joy of hearing the celestial music. There was a part of me that thought he might be impressed. I chuckle at that thought now, reminding myself that was before I knew Joseph very well. His response was, "Did you count the number of shards of clay?" Counting the broken bits of the pot had not occurred to me. I missed it. "Next time, count them. That will tell you what level of sound you reached."

Create Your Own Ceremony

Just as Joseph creates ceremonies, you can do the same, either by yourself or together with one or more friends. When creating spontaneous ceremonies, it is important to include the three universal elements of ceremony: *intention, sound,* and *movement*. Intention is the clear purpose of the ceremony and sets the theme and tone. The sound can be the blowing of breath, words, prayers, chanting, drumming, singing or music in whatever form. Movement may include dancing, walking, running, or even passing around a sacred object. Physical objects are often incorporated into ceremonies so that everyone, including those not used to thinking abstractly, can participate. Most children do not think in the abstract until they are around nine and some adults have difficulty doing so at any age. Take for example someone who is celebrating a new phase of their life. The simple act of using a doorway, a metaphor for entering or stepping into something new, would clearly illustrate the purpose of the ceremony.

When a long-time associate completed her graduate degree, a group of friends came together in my home to celebrate her accomplishment and new career. We lined up in two rows behind a doorway, creating a path for our friend. (In addition to being actual thresholds, doorways are also symbols for deep transitional passages.) She stood at the doorway with eyes closed and slowly moved backward one step at a time.

Starting with the present and regressing into the past, she silently reviewed the experiences, challenges, people and gifts which had led her to this moment. She stopped when she completed her reverie. Then, with eyes still closed, she walked forward to the doorway, blessing each experience she had just revisited. She paused, imagining, wondering, and visualizing what might lie ahead. When ready, she opened her eyes and stepped boldly across the threshold, empowered and excited about starting her new life.

Recently, I attended a ceremony for a friend facing major surgery. Everyone was asked to bring a small, yet significant stone. Each person, in turn, shared the story or special meaning of their stone and why they had chosen it. One stone had come from Egypt to bring ancient wisdom. Another stone, shaped like a heart, was found on the grounds of the Edgar Cayce camp site. One had been the good luck token during a woman's difficult transitional experience. Another was carefully selected by someone's grandchild as the *right one* to give her mother's friend. Still another stone carried the blessings of a healer and on the stories went. It was a heartfelt experience for all. A glass bowl filled to the brim with the precious stones, each carrying a special prayer, was carefully placed on the bedside table of our friend during her time in the hospital. It certainly brought comfort, for there is something reassuring about being in the presence of blessings.

The ceremonies we create for ourselves and others are as varied as the sacred moments we experience. Spontaneous ceremonies can celebrate the moment, honor an important crossroads, release the past, or call in new energy. They may be lively or sedate, playful or serious, simple or complex, short or long, profound, healing and life-changing. They contribute depth and dimension to our lives and open us to the transcendent.

The possibilities are endless, for every ceremony is a unique creation, crafted with imagination and love. Whatever the nature of the ceremony, what matters most is the intention to *get in touch with Higher Mind* and the willingness to *stay open to the radiance of light that allows us to see with childlike innocence.*

CHAPTER FOUR

CEREMONIAL DANCE EXPANDS OUR BEING

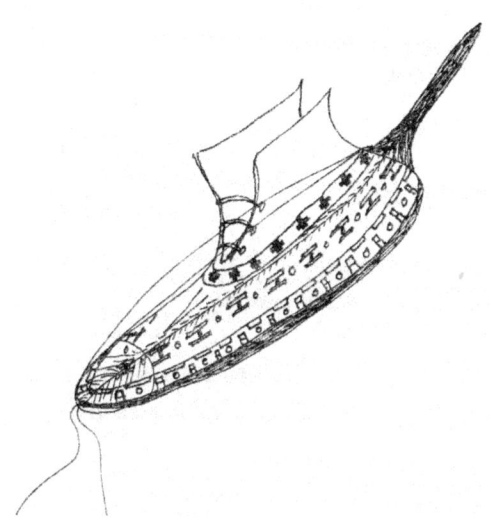

The Gift of Great Spirit

I HEARD A STORY OF ANONYMOUS ORIGIN RE-TOLD ON PUBLIC RADIO THAT GOES SOMETHING LIKE THIS:

It is said that a very long time ago before we had physical bodies we were just spirit, so we moved in our spirit form from one place to another, from one thing to another. We might have decided to go inside an oak tree, or a humming bird or a sunflower, and then leave whenever we wanted.

Because Great Spirit loved us so much, he decided to give us a very special gift, a physical body, so we could enjoy the Earth in a new way. In the beginning, we liked our bodies. We soon realized when we were in our bodies we could not remember our Spirit. So we left our bodies.

Seeing our dilemma Great Spirit thought, "I must do something so people will be happy staying in their bodies." He thought a long time about what that might be. Finally he said, "I know just the thing. I will give you dance and stories and song and then you will want to stay in your bodies because they will keep you connected to Spirit. "Once we had the gift of dance and stories and song, we never again needed to leave our bodies to remember Great Spirit Waa Maa Chi"

At a Sun Dance in 1983, Joseph was directed by Great Spirit to share with mankind sacred ceremonies for the healing of Mother Earth, individuals and all our relations. One of these ceremonies is the Drum Dance, a three-day fast with no food and no water (with occasional rest periods) where one dances to the rhythmic beat of drums and the singing of chants. It is an exquisite ceremony nuanced with layers of metaphor and meaning.

To understand ceremonial dance is to understand first of all that *God is breath, matter, and Spirit or waa-ma-chi in Tiwa. Waa is breath, or Spirit,* for without breath, our bodies would have no life. *Maa means to materialize, to manifest,* and as we breathe, we move or dance and create in the physical world. *And chi is the inspiration, the truth that feeds breath, matter, and movement.*

Dance is movement and learning takes place in movement; learning and movement complement each other. In Tiwa, movement means *to be able to see.* As soon as we move we have perceptual power, the capacity to look at fine detail and simultaneously perceive the larger whole. We change continually and progress to higher and higher states of consciousness. As we dance, the psyche expands so what we don't know at the beginning of the dance we have the awareness to know at the end of the dance. Perhaps we are revitalizing dormant neurons to accept more revelations.

Preparing for the Dance Ceremony

When dancers, drummers, chanters, and other participants of various kinds begin arriving at the dance site, they are met with hugs and warm welcomes. A sense of expectancy fills the air. Cooks gather in the kitchen to start preparing the celebratory feast which will take place when the dance is over. Chanters and drummers meet for last minute instructions. Dancers erect colorful tents of various shapes and sizes or lay out simple camp gear on open ground on the periphery of the location. A sweat lodge ceremony purifies and prepares them for the upcoming ceremony while the dance site, a sacred space always treated with reverence, gets its final touches.

The size of the dance area is approximately that of a football field. A row of tall wooden poles which bisects the entire length of the site is already in place. The poles are laced with string to which beautifully colored feathers are tied so the wind can dance the feathers as the dancers dance. And in the center of the field stands an especially tall pole where sacred objects are carefully arranged to help focus and ground all that transpires.

At the appointed moment, the drum calls the dancers to the dance. They take their places on either side of the line of poles and begin their individual rhythmic movements back and forth, their eyes focused on the feather blowing in the breeze. They dance for *awareness,* for *higher states of grace, higher states of being.* As the dancers move forward they give; as they move backwards they receive. Their movements reflect an alignment with a universal order, for the head, neck, eyes, arms, legs, and feet are metaphors for principle ideas that govern the cosmos. And so by dancing, they become increasingly receptive to Higher Mind and the guidance it gives.

The dancers begin to clear a path, symbolic of their path in life. Some dance barefoot. Others wear moccasins, sandals, or shoes of one kind or another. No matter what foot covering, the dancers long to touch deeply the earth and remember the language of the land.

Some are attired in colorful ceremonial garb; some wear simple clothing. The women wear long skirts, the men straight skirts or long pants. As the drum beat continues, they dance for the collective and they dance for themselves. The heart-beat of Mother Earth begins to take them deep within.

Accompanying the drummers is a group of chanters singing praises to God (Great Spirit). Their voices wash through the dancers' bodies, filling them with light, clearing old patterns and beliefs, opening them to new images, new insights and visions. Limitations are transcended. Consciousness expands and the prayers of the heart are sent skyward. Many arduous hours pass.

Slowly, an internal shift occurs until finally there comes a moment when *they* no longer dance. Something beyond themselves begins to *dance them. Their legs become the drum stick and the Earth the drum.*

Resistance to the Dance

As beautiful and exquisite as I now know the dance to be, I did not step readily or quickly into this particular ceremony. In fact, it took quite some time before I fell in love with it. I danced my first Drum Dance in the late 80s, not an easy three days, though the experience was quite energizing.

I did not feel compelled to do it again. So when the time came to dance the following year, I chose not to participate. After all, did I really *need* this experience? Not understanding the deeper levels of the dance, my reluctance was easy to rationalize. Joseph speaks about two minds: the *God mind* and the *rational mind*. At that moment, I was in the rational mind. The dance I would have attended began on Friday. That same evening, I went to bed as usual and was awakened from a deep sleep with a powerful dream.

In the dream, which felt like a visitation, I saw a group of Native American men sitting bare-chested in a circle with red blankets draped around their shoulders. Who are they? I didn't know who they were. Their presence was auspicious. No words were spoken, yet there was a sense of urgency about their appearance.

I knew instantly I was being called to the dance. There was no time to waste. Though it was still before dawn, I promptly jumped out of bed, loaded up my car with the barest of essentials and began the six-hour drive to the dance site in Pottstown, Pennsylvania. On arrival, I immediately joined in with the other dancers.

Sometime later, I asked Joseph about the men in red. He said they were the Council of Elders, the wisdom keepers of the Native American tradition. I was glad I had paid heed to them. It was sometime later when I realized the group which appeared in the dream were the same as the ones who gave Joseph the vision to build the Sound/Peace Chambers.

Conflict Resolved

It was a gift to be visited by the Elders. On the other hand, it brought to my attention an internal conflict which took some time to sort out. Since early childhood, I felt a strong loyalty to my Judeo-Christian background. One does not neglect a deep faith built on teachings and experiences from both exoteric and esoteric Christianity. It was and continues to be a deep river which runs through me.

I was familiar also with the references to the White Brotherhood by Edgar Cayce and others. They are the beings assigned to preserve and protect the mystery teachings of the Judeo-Christian tradition. So when confronted with the Council of Elders, it took some time to integrate what, in hindsight, seem obvious. My mental monkey-mind was stuck in the paradox of either-or-thinking believing I needed to choose one form or the other.

Quite out of the blue I asked Joseph: What is the connection between the Council of Elders and the White Brotherhood?" Joseph in his wisdom and gentleness said, "I have always wondered that myself, so I asked that same question. They are not the same and they are connected to the same Source."

Truth has a ring all its own. Of course. Obvious. It was not just the answer Joseph gave, but the grace in which he responded. Definitely, one of his finest attributes—and a response I will not forget. With that realization, I am comfortable with not one, but two deep rivers which run through me, knowing without any doubt their Source is one.

More Insights about the Dance

Though the Drum Dance lasts for three days, there is no preordained hour when it stops. When I asked Joseph how he knows when to end the dance, his answer was simple: when there is enough *gold dust* (a metaphor for light) coming off the dance site.

As people dance back and forth on their path, there comes a point in the dance when a gold disc appears over the head of each dancer and a golden light shines through their body. On the path where they have been dancing, there is gold dust. When there is enough gold dust collectively, the dance is ended. The gold light rises up into the clouds and comes down in the rain, showering the earth with awareness. *Light effectuates the continual evolution toward higher states of grace, higher states of being.*

It is one thing to hear a teaching and quite another to experience it first-hand. At the end of the third day of my third dance, I turned around to look back at the dance site. There was the gold dust Joseph had spoken of flowing through the dancers and on the paths where they had been dancing. It was breathtaking and affirmed that these dances are not performed solely on the personal level but have a much greater universal purpose. For we also dance for *the people,* the collective vibration.

Layers of Metaphors

Resistant as I was initially, I soon fell in love with the dance. I also understand why drum dancers are asked to commit to six dances (usually done once each year). The Drum Dance is layered and nuanced with so much meaning and metaphor that it takes many years to fully assimilate the entire experience. Furthermore, each dance affords its own gifts, so all six dances are required for the ceremony to be complete. The first dance brings the power of the unexpected. The next dance enables you to fall into creative, wonderful power. With the third dance, directions and opportunities open to you, and the fourth brings down ideas to cultivate. The fifth carries the light of the priesthood, and with the sixth dance, wisdom opens to you.

When we dance, rhythms and cadence change unexpectedly. We learn to respond without hesitation to the call of the drum. In so doing, we learn to be present, still, move, shift, and respond to whatever presents itself. For to dance is *to learn to dance in life.* As we dance, we also honor our existence as part of the greater whole, including the unfolding of the cosmos, and *become one sea of energy.*

Note:
  Enclosed is The Drum Dance schedule. Also, The United Nations letter I think you should have regarding The Peace Kivas around The World. Also, Now your Spirit is Also. And I'm sending you The St. Elizabeth Town College brochure.
        Just wanted to let you know That
The Synchronicity's seem to be unending. You know
                                    should know
many Elizabeth marlow. I think I finally starting to
it.   With Loving Blessings

              Joseph & Peggy Owens
                  4/11/89

CHAPTER FIVE

FEMININE ENERGY COMES FIRST: THE MASCULINE IS AN EXTENSION OF THE FEMININE

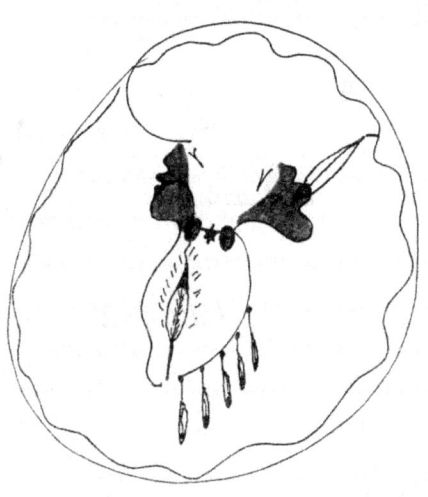

Coming to Terms

ONE OF THE INITIAL CHALLENGES IN TEACHING WITH JOSEPH was coming to terms with my part and place in working with him. To do that, I needed to know more about his understanding of masculine and feminine energies. I wanted to be assured I was not stepping into a patriarchy since that would be a step backwards. Honoring women and the feminine energy is of high value, not only to me personally, but to the many friends and groups of women I have known and been connected with.

It was important to learn that in his mother's tribe, the Utes, women select a partner during the Bear Dance and whoever they choose must dance with them. It was also important to discover that some of Joseph's teachers had been medicine women.

In the Pueblo tradition, women (the feminine, the round or circle energy) are in charge of the Pueblo households, which are basically square. The men (the masculine or square energy) have their medicine teachings in underground kivas, which are circular. One way either gender learns its opposite or less dominant function is through the shapes of the architectural forms they inhabit. The concept is fascinating.

In ceremonial dances, men and women dance together, but they dance different forms. In one dance the women hold sprigs of evergreen, a healing energy, at the heart level. With elbows bent, arms extended sideways and palms turned upwards, moving gracefully with the rhythm of the drums, they enact the metaphor of expressing from the heart and bringing balance. The men have evergreen tied around their arms, but instead of arms outstretched to the side, they dance in place and extend their arms forward in a directed energy. The energies of both women and men, the feminine and masculine, are honored and recognized as different, yet each has its special place.

A Few Adjustments

To say teaching with Joseph required a few adjustments is an understatement. On a humorous note, Joseph always insisted I drive when we went somewhere together. Driving is not something I am good at or even particularly enjoy. My preference is to sit in the passenger seat and take in the surroundings, rather than having to focus on the road. Maybe that was the whole point. I needed more *focus*.

I recall vividly an experience when I was driving totally distracted, lost in an elevated conversation with Joseph. In fact, it would be fair to say I was in an altered state—definitely not a good place to be when one is behind the wheel. We were riding along on an open road in the vast, treeless terrain of central New Mexico in an area where one seldom sees another car, when suddenly we heard the high-pitched wail of a siren and saw flashing lights in the rear view mirror. We pulled over and the policeman sauntered up to our car.

"Ma'am, do you know how fast you were going?" "No sir, I don't," was my honest response.

"I have you clocked at ninety miles per hour." I was stunned. "Officer, I live in Virginia where we seldom experience such beautiful wide-open landscapes. I got lost in the vastness of New Mexico."

In hindsight, the excuse was totally lame. Luckily, the policeman had mercy on me and reduced the violation on the ticket to speeding, rather than reckless driving. He then proceeded to instruct me on how to speed without getting caught.

"If you want to speed," he continued, "you should get behind another car that is speeding." I assured the officer that was not my intent and thanked him for the tip. Maybe I was hoping at some unconscious level this demonstration of reckless driving would surely relieve me of my role as designated driver. It did not. The driving assignment continued, though thereafter I did keep the speed in check.

Being the driver was only one of many adjustments. I was used to teaching on my own or co-teaching with persons where we divided up the segments of programs more or less equally. With Joseph it was a totally different situation. We came together with me knowing almost nothing about Native American traditions Not that he is limited exclusively to that form, but his teachings are unequivocally grounded in his tradition. Even if I were to learn quickly, we would never be *equal* in that sense.

Sometimes it was an inner struggle to take a place alongside someone who travels in and out of multiple dimensions. Comparisons are often a form of judgment based on insecurity. I soon learned to replace those thoughts by seeing Joseph as someone who demonstrates the infinite possibilities available to any and all of us. Teaching with him required acceptance of who I am and what I had to offer.

On more than one occasion, Joseph said, "You just don't get it. It's about energy and what you bring and who you are." How easy it is to become overly concerned with ego needs. It was more important that our combination of energies serve the group.

When I recall our many vision quests, a plethora of images and memories come to mind, many of which are inspiring and profound. There is one memory, though, I remember now with a chuckle. It was the *one* moment in all the time spent with Joseph when he was visibly off-center.

It happened when a particular vision quest was over and my rented car was lopsided due to a flat tire. Not only was my tire flat, but a vision quest participant from Norway simultaneously discovered her tire was flat as well. For Joseph, changing the tire of the Norwegian was not a problem. Changing two tires, though, was more than he bargained for. He was annoyed to deal once again with stubborn lug nuts. As he picked up the tire iron, he shot me a chilling look. (It is refreshing to know that even cosmic dancers can, on occasion, become irritated.) I am pleased to report

that by the time he had installed the spare tire, his mood had shifted and the twinkle was back again in Joseph's eyes.

On still another occasion, when a vision quest was scheduled to last for three days, Joseph decided after only two days that the experience was complete. Mystics go by different rules. Predictable schedules and clear time-lines just aren't a part of someone who is inner-directed. I had the uncomfortable task of gathering everyone from their sites and routing them back to the Sound/Peace Chamber. Of particular concern were the participants who had come all the way from Europe and who might not be able to make last-minute sleeping arrangements. Happily, the abrupt change in plans was not a problem for anyone. If Joseph said the experience was over, then he was guided to do so and that was fine with them. We were grateful to have such a flexible group. If they could be present and adapt so gracefully to change, then indeed the vision quest had come to a successful conclusion.

As time went by, teaching with Joseph became effortless and spontaneous. And when my book *Jumping Mouse*, based on a traditional Plains Indian story, was released, Joseph suggested we do programs based on the book's theme—the journey to the sacred mountain. Quite a gracious gesture. I chuckle remembering one particular experience during the *Jumping Mouse* retreat.

We were with our group on a mesa in New Mexico. When I finished teaching a segment of the story, we took a short break. In the interim Joseph suggested we stop for the day. From my perspective, we needed one more segment. No sooner had the words come out of my mouth than loud thunder broke the stillness of the day. I quickly said, "And the thunder beings agree." With that, Joseph immediately nodded his head, for the thunder beings always have the final word. I smiled broadly . . . It was affirming to have support from the thunder beings.

Mysteries of Darkness

In Joseph's tradition, *the feminine comes first, followed by the masculine, which is an extension of the feminine.* That metaphor is rendered beautifully in the three-day Drum Dance. In the pre-dawn hours of the dance, dancers are awakened with a gentle, intermittent tapping of the drum. They get dressed silently and prepare for a full day of dancing. *Darkness before dawn is positive, not negative, for the darker the light the purer it is. To get that purity, our eyes must be open. Then, that black light will carry us in the days or weeks ahead.*

At some level, we innately know the deeper mystery of the pre-dawn hours. It is the place of the deep feminine, where we learn to appreciate and trust the unknown.

One of my most treasured childhood memories occurred during those early hours. My brother John and I awoke very early, when the Earth was still in darkness. With the help of our mother who was in on the plan, we got dressed amid whispers, tiptoed quietly out of the house and made a run for our father's car. We quickly tumbled into the back seat with muffled giggles and crouched on the floor, where we waited excitedly with great anticipation. A few minutes later, daddy made his way out of the house, opened the car door, positioned himself behind the wheel, and started the car. We could hardly contain ourselves. We were hunched down behind the driver's seat, *shh*-ing each other to keep quiet. After we had driven a few miles from our home, we jumped up yelling in unison, "Surprise! Surprise!"

"Oh!" he exclaimed, beaming with great delight. "Are you back there? I didn't know that. Well, I guess now I'll just have to take you with me to the farm!" which of course was exactly what we wanted. Our farm was a seven mile drive from our home, where the unexpected was always present, especially when it was still dark and all nature was just beginning to awaken. It never occurred to us then that maybe, just maybe, daddy was not really surprised. On that day, the association of excitement, mystery, and wonder were forever linked to the pre-dawn hours. It is still my favorite time of the day.

Metaphors of the Feminine and Masculine

At all Drum Dance sites, women and men sleep in separate locations. In Pottstown, Pennsylvania, where many of us have danced, the women camp up on a hill and the men sleep at the foot of the hill. When everyone is ready, the women, dressed in skirts (these are circular, a metaphor for the feminine) and arrayed in other ceremonial garb, line up two by two and come down the hill singing *klee whey ney,* Tiwa for "feminine." The delicate sound of female voices singing in two and three part harmony as the women gracefully descend the hill in the quiet early morning hours is enchanting.

As we enter the dance site, we disappear as women. We are really not there. No one is there. We become feminine energy, or descending light. Over time, we learn to see beyond physical form so we can see a different kind of vibration.

The men are stretched out in a line across the dance site lying on their backs with eyes closed. As the women walk past each man, two women, each carrying feathers, one by one gently brush the head and chest of the man as they pass. The feathers became a magical wand. The descending light touches the masculine with light. As the light is given, one by one each man stands up, indicating he has received what has been given and is ready to respond.

Think of the feminine as a hollow reed, a flute, open and receptive to the descending light which enters from above. The feelings, body sensations, insights and intuitions which defy the rational mind are all a part of what we call the feminine. The feminine, the *being* energy, gives to the masculine, or *doing* energy, which directs and acts on what has been given.

In the Greek myth of Psyche, a similar teaching is presented. A turning point in the story comes when Psyche stands over Eros, her husband, with a lantern in one hand and a knife in the other, ready to kill the 'monster.' Up to this point in the story, Psyche is in an unconscious relationship. She does not know herself, and she does not know the man she married. When she holds the light over Eros, she sees who he truly is. Why, he is not a monster after all. For the first time, she recognizes his beauty and strength, which is also her disowned male side.

The light and the knife are two important metaphors in the journey of every soul. The light, the feminine illumination, insight, and inspiration come first. The knife is the active, male energy. Sometimes we have an inspired idea, a new realization, and we fail to pick up the knife to act on it. So having the light alone is not enough. Likewise, the knife without the light doesn't work, either, for then we are too impulsive. We act on whims which do not originate from a clear source or we misuse the knife. We project onto others. We hurt with words, thoughts, or deeds, rather than using the knife to cut ourselves free from patterns that no longer serve. When we go back to the Source (or the Light) whatever change or action we take then is not directed by impulse, but rather by intuition.

Feminine and Masculine in Harmony

When one is unified, there is a graceful dance between the feminine and masculine energy. A particular incident comes to mind which demonstrates the natural flow between these two energies. Joseph and I were scheduled to teach a weekend seminar in Virginia Beach. As was always the plan when Joseph came to the Beach, I was to pick him up at the Norfolk airport and bring him back to my home where he stayed during his visits. On Thursday afternoon I got a call around five o'clock. It was Joseph. I was surprised to hear from him since he is not a 'phone person' and was scheduled to fly in the next day, or at least that is what I thought. The conversation went something like this:

"Hello?" "Hi," said Joseph.

"It's good to hear from you. Looking forward to seeing you tomorrow."

"Well, actually I'm here." "You're here? I thought you were coming in tomorrow." "No," he said quite calmly. "It's today." When I got off the plane I looked for you. Then, I got my luggage and still didn't see you. So, I went outside and I saw this bus that said Holiday Inn. I have always wondered what the Holiday Inn was like. So I got on the bus and I am here now."

"You're at the Norfolk Holiday Inn?" I was stunned. "Well, what are you doing? "Oh, I'm getting ready to have some soup."

"Do you want some company?" "Sure." I immediately jumped in my car and drove too fast to the Holiday Inn where we shared hearty bowls of soup, much laughter, and fascinating conversation, none of which related to the airport incident. That day and in numerous other situations is how Joseph responds. Always present. He quickly adapts and shifts to whatever life presents. He does not waste energy being in the *monkey mind*, interpreting and speculating obsessively about what this or that meant, or what should or should not have happened. There is no blame, ever. When one is unified and not stuck in the duality of either-or-thinking, then one moves effortlessly from feminine awareness to masculine action. One stays present and asks only one question: *what does the moment ask*? The answer, in this case, was simple. Go get some food!

After our meal, I said, "Do you want to come back to the house now? "No, that's okay. I'm set up here now. If you could pick me up around nine, that would be good." The incident was never brought up again. And needless to say, I arrived at the Holiday Inn *on time* to pick up Joseph the next morning.

CHAPTER SIX

WE ARE NOT HERE

It has been said that we are the Spirit of "many faces" so that life can enter each moment and face up to it.

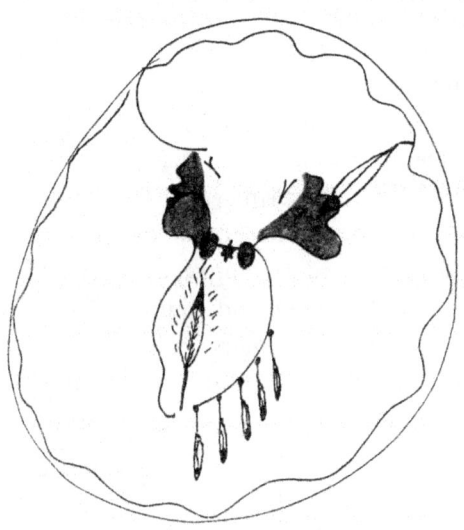

Higher Mind Moves through Us

To fully understand the teachings of Joseph Rael, it is important to know something about Tiwa, the language Joseph heard and spoke growing up in Picuris Pueblo. Because Tiwa is his first language, he still thinks in Tiwa and silently translates English and Spanish to his native tongue when someone is speaking to him. The spiritual truths underlying this language are an integral part of the deep wisdom of his people and are at the very core of his teaching

For Joseph, language *is an enormous ball of whirling energies which came from the being of goodness*. Great Creator made the different languages from this ball, each with resonating qualities of goodness, and each with its own specific vibration different from the others.

Historians tell us that sometime around 1300 C.E. the Anasazi dispersed from their cliff dwellings in Mesa Verde. Some went to the Hopi and Zuni communities. Thousands of other traveled east to New Mexico's Rio Grande Valley, which is now New Mexico. They spoke various dialects or tongues, one of which was Tiwa. Like their ancestors before them, the Tiwa-speaking people built adobe houses and practiced desert agriculture. The Spanish arriving in the sixteenth century called these people *Pueblos,* the Spanish word for *town*. Today, Tiwa is spoken at Picuris, Taos, Sandia and Isleta Pueblos in New Mexico.

Joseph says we become the language we speak and to a great extent, language decides the vibration a person carries. Tiwa carries a cosmic vibration, If a person speaks that language, they embody that resonance. What is especially relevant about Tiwa is that it is a *verb* language. If one grows up in a language which is primarily verbs, it is then understood that as a people, we do not create action. Action, or life, comes *through* us.

In contrast, virtually all modern languages are noun/pronoun languages. They tend to identify with the ego and "thingify." To those of us from noun/pronoun cultures, Joseph suggests we internally add the *ing* suffix to our names. In groups, he will sometimes ask people to address each other by their name with *ing added* on the end. Robert becomes Roberting and Helen is Helening.

The effect of doing this over the course of even half a day is quite profound. For when we experience ourselves as an *ing* being, our perception changes. Automatically, we are more receptive to Higher Mind moving through us. Once we give up ego, we begin to open to the infinite wisdom of the universe. The reason cosmic dancers attain higher levels of consciousness is because they put ego aside to such an extent that a higher group mind works through them and they become a participant in that mind.

For Tiwa speakers, this world is a place of illusion called *maya*. One of the ways he or she learns this is through heightened states of consciousness experienced during ceremonies and dances. They know they are present and not present at the same time. Their mind is there and not just their mind—there is also Higher Mind, the creative intelligence of the universe which thinks through them.

The Tiwa speaker practices *not being*. It is the place where God hides. Buddhists call it emptiness, *shunyata*. If we don't exist in a conditioned egoic state of consciousness, new information and new knowledge can enter. Otherwise, the ego will limit higher wisdom because the ego thinks it knows everything and what it knows is sufficient to continue its life.

The place of *not being,* or openness, is not nothingness. For all creativity, clarity and universal knowledge arise from this luminous space.

Appearing and Disappearing

When you watch a slide show, one slide is projected on the screen. Then it is removed and the screen goes blank for a moment, followed by another slide. There is form, no-form, and then form again. When we go to the cinema we are still seeing individual images, but now the images are flashed on the screen in a much quicker sequence. Our brain merges these images, so we experience the motion picture as one uninterrupted story.

Quantum physicist Greg Braden says our everyday reality operates in a way similar to that of a movie. For example, when we watch a runner racing down a track, we perceive one continuous, uninterrupted movement. In reality, that is not what is happening. Our brain has merged together the brief tiny bursts of energy, or light, called *quanta*. Thus, what we consider to be "reality" is not so real or solid after all. The runner, in actuality, is appearing and disappearing. So in truth, *we are not here*, at least not in the way we think we are.

In the emptiness, in those *between spaces* beyond form, beyond anything you can think about yourself, is where we experience the source field from which all of our energies emerge. For a miniscule fraction of a second we are formless, in the loving embrace of pure spirit. Just as quickly we return to form and the material world. So in truth, we are appearing and disappearing, moving from form to the formless world, over and over again.

I asked Joseph, "Since we return to the light again and again, why do we not progress more quickly?" His answer was, "Because we are so stuck."

Most of us have not yet learned to see the bursts of light as the runner goes down the track, since they are too rapid for the untrained eye. When one can slow the mind down sufficiently, one sees the quanta. Then, one can also see the possible future of an individual in slices of light as happened when Joseph glimpsed my future at our first meeting in the woods, as well as see global visions of what is to come. How extraordinary to be living at a point in time when what the mystics have always known is now being confirmed by science.

Form and No-Form

There is no better way to understand the principle of appearing and disappearing, of form and no form, than to *dance* it. We did just that with a group during a five day retreat program in Colorado. In this particular dance, there were two lines of dancers. The line on the right side represented daytime (the sun) and that on the left nighttime (the moon). During the dance, each side crosses over to the other side. When the dancers cross over, there is a moment when day becomes night and the night becomes day. The no-form becomes the form and the form becomes the no-form. It all occurs at the speed of light, 186,282 miles per second. Yet, the observer thinks he is watching the whole scenario of one continuous story, when in truth dancers are appearing and disappearing, being form and formless. Quantum mechanics says we come from light. So for a split second we were the light, and that light exists momentarily, disappears and then reappears again.

It is possible that when we danced we may not have completely understood *what* we were dancing, or if we did, we did so only in part. To fully comprehend that we are constantly entering the formless reality of divine presence where all is purified and resolved and returning immediately to the material world of form, is a great deal to absorb. Perhaps it doesn't matter whether we know it with our rational mind or not. For when we dance the metaphors of universal consciousness, teachings bypass the linear mind and are translated non-verbally into the very cells of the body.

We Are Not Here

That *we are not here* is an essential concept to understand and integrate at the cellular level. We long to experience first-hand the importance of putting ego, our little self, aside so we may be directed increasingly by Higher Mind. Then this teaching is no longer an abstract concept, but one which is practical, real, and applicable in our life, as the following story illustrates.

On one trip to Picuris Pueblo, our vans made a stop at a gas station/roadside stand not far from Picuris. While the vans were getting gas, our group had time to stretch a little and purchase fruit and snacks. Little attention was given to who bought what. Probably no one noticed Joseph

leaving with a small brown bag filled with something he purchased at the stand.

A short time later we made another stop. This time we pulled into a look-out area with a scenic overview. The winding Rio Grande River was at our feet and the graceful Saingre de Cristo "Blood of Christ" mountain range stood majestically before us.

As we stood enjoying the magnificent convergence of river and mountain, Joseph told us we were standing on land which in earlier times belonged to Picuris. *This is sacred land. It is here where my people go through these mountains when they make their transition to the other side. Some of you might be more familiar with the concept of going through a tunnel when one dies and transitions to the other side. The veil to the other side is thin here. So pay attention. It is easy to communicate with loved ones who have gone before.*

Almost immediately I distinctly felt the familiar presence of my father who had succumbed to cancer some years earlier. Just as I was absorbing the impact of this profound moment, Joseph spontaneously walked towards where I was standing and without saying anything, gave me a brown bag filled with peaches. With that gesture my tears began to flow.

During the final stages of my father's illness, he asked the hospital staff to remove the IV's which were keeping him alive so he could come home.

As the doctors explained, "Without IV's, most people in your father's condition won't live longer than three days. Because Mr. Marlow is a little 'different' we don't know how long he may last."

As it turned out, he lived nine days. My father wanted to make his final transition at home in familiar surroundings with his family, his home and his garden—what he loved and valued most.

During my last visit with daddy, he asked my mother, "Do we have any peaches? Give Betty (the name he called me) some peaches."

My mother promptly went to the kitchen and put peaches in a paper sack, returned to the bedroom and handed them to my father. In turn, he gave them to me. What an appropriate last gift. My father had a generous spirit and was always giving. In this case, he gave something beautiful, real and simple from Mother Earth, values for me to carry and remember.

Joseph didn't know the story about my last moments with my father. So giving the peaches was not a conscious decision. In that moment, the ego which is stuck in the many forms, beliefs, and patterns of the material world disappeared. Higher Mind, the creative intelligence of the universe was moving through him. Such moments happen to all of us . . . *when we are not here.*

CHAPTER SEVEN

DON'T GET STUCK IN FORM

Beyond Form

*I*F THERE IS ONE STATEMENT WHICH IS REPEATED BY JOSEPH MORE THAN ANY OTHER it is *don't get stuck in form*. A particular incident proved to be a vivid enactment of this teaching. Several former students of the late Sun Bear (Ojibwa medicine man) came to participate in a sweat lodge ceremony. They arrived early enough to help build the lodge and proudly began to tell Joseph about the many years they had built sweat lodges for Sun Bear. Joseph nodded respectfully and said, "Put four doors in the sweat lodge," and walked away.

Anyone who has ever done a sweat knows four doors are seldom, if ever, used. Usually there is only one door positioned on the east side of the lodge which is the place where wisdom enters. So when Joseph issued his unexpected directive, the students were bewildered. They said nothing though their faces registered disbelief. It was a form they had never used.

Nevertheless, they did indeed build a lodge according to Joseph's specifications. That day, and that day only, we experienced a sweat lodge ceremony with four doors. The teaching was *don't get stuck in form*. Form is important and has its place and ultimately all form is to be transcended.

Whether it is a Native American sweat lodge, Catholic Mass, or the Jewish Shabbat, the only thing which ultimately matters is what is awakened within the self. *For all forms are used to take us to the place beyond form.*

More Than One Form

It is not surprising that after a year or so co-teaching with Joseph, I would experience my own challenges with the principle of not getting stuck in form. It was a new concept for me. Once we learn something helpful it must be applied in life to make it ours.

It all began in Manhattan where I was to give a lecture and seminar for the Whole Life Times Expo. A dinner invitation from a longtime friend would come to be the more significant reason for my being in New York.

As my friend Mary explained, it would be 'sing-for-your-supper' event in an upscale penthouse apartment. In other words, we would be wined and dined royally. In turn, we were expected to participate in lively discussions. *Wonderful! Just my kind of evening.*

Soon after arriving at the Park Avenue address, twelve or so dinner guests of varied backgrounds were seated at a long table and interesting conversation began quite effortlessly. The primary reason for the occasion was to honor Dr. Jerry Rubin, a psychiatrist who had just published a new book on guided imagery. Seated on my right was a psychologist, with whom we soon engaged in good conversation.

At some point during the second or third course, my attention was drawn to my left where Dr. Rubin was seated. He turned to me and without any preliminary remarks said quite unexpectedly, "You had a visionary experience when you were very young, didn't you?"

I was somewhat taken back. After all, until that moment this man was a complete stranger. And besides, only a handful of people knew of the vision I had experienced at the age of five when insights of my future were shown.

"Yes. How did you know?" "I read it in your face," he replied.

"Is that an ability you were born with?" "No. I learned it from Colette, my teacher in Israel." With the mention of the name Colette a rush of energy surged throughout my entire body. For a woman, the body is the oldest source of wisdom. The potent energy that coursed through my being was indicative of a strong resonance with this woman I had not yet met.

"You should go to Israel and meet her." Without hesitation I said, "Yes,

I'd like that very much." Immediately, my mind raced to figure out the logistics. After teaching in Germany, I could travel to Israel. The great distance between the two countries not to mention the history between the two countries didn't seem to register. Nothing mattered at the moment except the clear knowing that meeting Colette was important. Dr. Rubin said matter-of-factly, "Just send her your picture and a letter explaining why you want to come."

I returned to Virginia Beach and posted both the picture and the letter which Jerry suggested I write. Several months later I found myself knocking at Colette's door in Jerusalem and hearing a thick Israeli accent, "*Kom enn.*"in the background.

An assistant ushered me through a gallery–style hallway lined with pictures of what appeared to be family, friends and students. She ushered me into a living room where my eyes went directly to an elegant, diminutive lady, a Helen Hayes look-alike with graying upswept hair. She sat propped up against colorful cushions, her upper body draped in a soft, lilac-colored shawl. I was introduced to Colette and took my seat in a straight-backed chair directly in front of her. Even at first glance it was obvious she decidedly was a woman with deep wisdom and an enormously beautiful spirit.

Every day for nine days I found my way to her home on King David Street. With this being my third trip to Israel, recollections of mysterious memories were stirred. A wealth of feelings, scenes, experiences, insights, and connections from other times resurfaced with an intensity which was somewhat overpowering.

At the end of my nine days in Jerusalem, Colette generously offered to continue to be my teacher. I was pleased with this proposal, especially since I am not Jewish and she is quite selective about whom she teaches. During our time together, there had been moments when going into the depths with Colette were both challenging and helpful. She was clear and to the point.

The thought of being under the tutelage of a wise woman had a warm feel to it. I welcomed the opportunity of being mentored by a Jewish mystic and the new perspective this experience would bring. However, her offer was conditional upon my agreement not to study with anyone else. After careful thought, my decision was to become Colette's student to the exclusion of all other teachers. It would also mean traveling back and forth to Israel.

When I returned home, I phoned Joseph to share my experience with Colette and explain that I would not be able to work with him anymore. He respectfully accepted my decision and that was that . . . or would have been, except early the next morning I was awakened with a resounding inner voice . . . *No, that will not work. I cannot be limited to one form, not at this point in my life.*

Truth has a resonance all its own. At such times there is no equivocation, no doubt to raise its head. I called Joseph to tell him of the change. There was no long discussion and no drama. He was pleased and welcomed me back. However, the confirmation as to whether I had passed this initiation did not come until a great deal of time had elapsed.

Some years later a phone call came from a Canadian woman whom I did not know. She had just returned from Israel where she had been studying with this very same Colette. While there, she attended Colette's eightieth birthday party. She proceeded to describe the cake for the celebration which was made in the shape of a white buffalo. That was significant since some years after my time with Colette, I had written a book entitled *Jumping Mouse* based on a Plains Indian story. In the book, Colette was anthropomorphically animated as the wise *buffalo* who helps Jumping Mouse on his way to the sacred mountain. At her birthday party, she presented copies of the Hebrew translation of *Jumping Mouse* to each of her grandchildren. I was delighted with the news and the validation from a higher plane that this initiation had indeed been passed. Life, the ultimate teacher, has a way of confirming wise choices.

From the One to the Many

We are at a time in our history when we recognize many systems, many cosmologies, and many forms, each with teachings which have the capacity to take us to the formless realm. Everything is cross-culturally variable and with so many paths available, one may wish to embrace various forms.

Joseph Campbell encourages any spiritual seeker to first delve deeply into one form before opening to others. Born into a Roman Catholic family, Campbell felt he had completed his study of Catholicism by the age of twenty-eight. Only then was he ready to begin an earnest exploration of the similarities and differences between various traditions. His journey is a manifestation of the ancient spiritual precept: *from the one we open to the many*. If we fully understand one tradition, we can then embrace others.

"Tell me Your Secret"

The idea of being totally grounded in one form and yet open to other forms was profoundly illustrated in 1990 in Dharansala, a remote town in Northern India, when an unprecedented dialogue took place between Jews and Tibetan Buddhists. There, these two religiously and culturally disparate traditions, seemingly worlds apart, came together and found common ground. A primary unifying factor was that both groups had faced lengthy persecutions and the imminent destruction of their traditions and their people—most recently the Buddhists during the Cultural Revolution and the Jews during the Holocaust.

The Dalai Lama reached outside his Buddhist form and turned to the Jewish people for help. "Tell me your secret," he said, "the secret of Jewish spiritual survival in exile." In a thoroughly compelling book, *The Jew in the Lotus* author Rodger Kamenetz records the open exchange between the Dalai Lama and a group of Jewish spiritual leaders. (Rodger coincidentally also studied with Colette).

At the Lama's request, the discussion would include teachings about Kabbalah and Jewish meditation. In turn he would respond to questions about Buddhist teachings and practices. In the course of the dialogue, both sides found common ground in each other's seemingly divergent traditions as well as new points of view to consider, because all forms, be they of Eastern or Western philosophy, exist to take us ultimately beyond form.

Thunder Calling

A most dramatic and tangible experience of going *beyond form* occurred for those of us who were participants in a rare thunder calling ceremony. This experience was particularly significant since Joseph, who belongs to the Thunder-Calling Clan has not performed this ceremony for at least thirty years.

Thunder-calling is an ancient rite originating in a time when people sustained their sacred connection to the Great Creator and knew the language of the land. They were in harmony with all life and knew the language of the sky, rain, clouds, lighting and the thunder-beings.

According to Joseph, a powerful inner force guided him to conduct this particular ceremony at this particular time and invite a selected group of twenty persons to participate in the five-day event. When we arrived at the site of the Colorado Sound/Peace Chamber, we could not imagine the magnitude of the paradigm shift about to occur.

This particular chamber is an elliptical structure measuring about thirty feet at its widest point with a ladder inside providing access to the flat roof. All twenty of us spent several days enhancing the exterior and interior of the chamber. Together we added our energies to the natural beauty already present in and around the chamber. We stripped the bark off a fallen cottonwood tree and laid its boughs against the outer wall and gathered sage and cedar to place inside.

We moved in silence and acted with one mind, as if part of a beautifully choreographed dance. There is true peace in working in harmony with others, of sensing right timing and right action, of knowing when to do what. We also fasted, drinking only a mixture of blue corn meal (awareness) and water (light).

On the fourth day of the experience, Joseph announced without fanfare that the next day at two o'clock in the afternoon, we would *call down thunder*. An important piece to this story is his foster mother was the one who told Joseph the day and time the thunder calling would happen.

Though Joseph never had anything but respectful comments to share about his foster mother, his brothers told a different story. They said she was relentless in demanding Joseph to work unreasonably long and hard hours. Even so, he obeyed and did exactly what he was told to do. He accepted the situation as it was without needing it to be anything else. Through it all, Joseph avoided blame and stayed open to Higher Mind. The very person who was so challenging, in the end was the one who was there for Joseph. *This is a major lesson for all of us*. No wonder Joseph has earned the status of Thunder-Caller and a person in our time who can call in thunder!

The chances of a thunder storm or even a drizzle seemed slim at best for there was a drought that season and there was no forecast for rain. The earth was barren, parched and cracked. And besides, is it even possible to call down thunder? If one is limited to or stuck in the form of a three dimensional world and the laws of cause-and-effect which seemingly govern this reality, it is not possible. When one is in harmony with the spiritual laws of the universe and the vastness of its creative intelligence, then what we consider miraculous or impossible becomes possible.

Each Thunder Caller had a sizable stone selected from the bed of a shallow creek running nearby. The stone would keep them connected to the Mother energy and was theirs to use during the five days. On the fifth day, eight of us (four men and four women to keep the energy balanced) were asked to stand together in a line out in front of the group and call down thunder.

Eight persons were used because eight is the number of manifestation. Joseph asked us to lift our arms holding our river rocks high above our heads and then lower the rocks back down to the ground again. We were told once this same motion was repeated five times (five being the number of movement and infinite possibilities) we would hear the sound of thunder.

As eight of us took our places in a clearing, I looked up at the very blue, very clear sky and noticed there was not a single cloud. Not even a hint of a cloud. It would have been easy to doubt at this point. We began the ritual of lifting the rocks and bringing them back down to the earth. The second time we raised the rocks high over our heads, a few clouds began to form. Where did they come from? Seemingly out of nowhere. We continued, and even more clouds appeared. Somewhere between the fourth and fifth cycle of raising and lowering our rocks, and as if on cue, we heard the unmistakable sound of thunder rolling across the sky.

It was faint at first and grew increasingly louder and more distinct and powerful as it approached. I felt a rush of energy! As rain drops began to fall the sky was awash with light. It was a baptism and a showering of blessings. From that day forward, we are Thunder Callers. We have a new-found connection with the vibration of sound and our perception of reality has shifted permanently.

After the ceremony, we removed everything we had gathered and had placed so meticulously in and around the Sound/Peace Chamber. We returned it to its original natural state. One of the more poignant moments was walking down to the creek and giving our rocks back to the water beings. For a brief moment, there was a nostalgic longing to hold onto the beauty of the experience by keeping our rocks. That was not to be. Our deeper selves knew we no longer need the outer form—the decorated chamber or even a rock—now that the teaching of the ceremony had been internalized.

In a similar way, the Buddhist monks ceremoniously create elaborate sand mandalas and then dismantle them. Each mandala has a particular theme which is decided upon before proceeding. The making of the mandala is done silently while enraptured onlookers watch hour upon hour as intricate designs of magnificent colors are interlaid meticulously in sand. No sooner is the design complete than the monks brush the sand back toward the center where all colors run together. The sand is then scooped up, placed in small parcels and given to those who have witnessed the ceremony. Any remaining sand is taken to a nearby body of water. The rite reminds us of the impermanence of life: *Don't get stuck in form; All that exists is the eternal now.*

Beyond Form on a Personal Level

As individuals, we must ask ourselves: *What is the form (thoughts, emotions, beliefs, patterns) which may have served me in the past, but no longer serves us now?* Perhaps we are stuck in the role of victim, rescuer, pleaser, caregiver, and controller. Or we may be trapped in one or more of what Joseph calls the five major impediments: jealousy, anger, greed, mental obscuration (confused thinking and rigid thinking.)

We may also be saddled with beliefs that no longer serve us. We may be afraid that life will not support us, or think we need to be right, believe others are responsible for our happiness, or insist we are *entitled* to something different than what is. Attachment to form produces suffering.

Instead, we ask ourselves is there another way to perceive our situation? When the Koshare clown climbs the pole at Picuris, he sees life from another perspective—through the lens of Higher Mind. It is the same lens that changes our perception.

According to the medicine wheel, when we are *stuck in form*, we are in the South, the place of duality. To move to another position on the medicine wheel, we create movement. This can be accomplished by making even the smallest of changes in daily routine, such as taking a different route to work. Such a change may be minor but it refreshes us, frees our spirit, and moves our energy.

We can also interrupt and overcome "stuck" thinking by doing something radically different, out of character, ridiculous even. Like having ice cream for breakfast. Or taking your dishes for a ride in the car. Consider going by yourself on a vacation to a place you have never been. Decide to take singing lessons even if you think you can't sing. Think outside the box. The possibilities are endless. .

One very organized and predicable lady decided to make a big change. Contrary to her usual habits, she put on jeans, a black leather jacket and took a ride on a motorcycle! In another situation, a middle-aged woman recovering from a difficult and unwanted divorce decided to give herself a month long retreat. Rather than traveling to a specified retreat location and spending money beyond her means, she made a practical decision to create a quiet haven within the confines of her own home.

During her retreat, she planned to take extended walks in nature, play soothing music, read books (there had been no time to read), enjoy silence, meditate, and journal private thoughts. To be certain she would not be interrupted during her self-imposed solitude, she asked friends and her grown children not to call unless there was an emergency. She even boldly moved her mattress into the living room. She could then do something she had never done before—sleep on the floor in front of the fireplace. She was definitely breaking form.

At an appointed hour, she walked confidently from room to room, ringing a loud bell and proclaiming in a clear voice, "Hear ye, hear ye, the retreat of (giving her name) is about to begin." *Since our outer landscape reflects our inner landscape, if we change our outer world, our inner world shifts also.*

On a broader, more universal note, we are invited to heed the universal call which resonates so deeply at this time: *Go beyond the illusive form of separateness and remember we are one tribe, one people cohabitating together on this one small planet we call Earth.*

CHAPTER EIGHT

WHAT WE THINK WE KNOW IS NOT WHAT IS

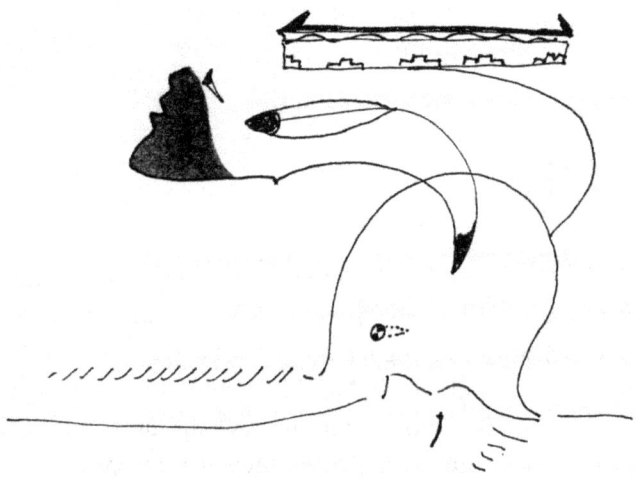

Perceptual Reality is in a State of Impermanence

According to Joseph, this universe is only one of many more universes, or planes of existence. It is only here on this plane that we have the opportunity to appreciate the *beauty of perception*, which he doesn't believe is available in any other realm, for *this is the plane where we learn about perception and attain a higher level of understanding of what is 'real'* will be challenged as the following narrative illustrates.

Picture for a moment a small caravan of vehicles proceeding south from Santa Fe to Bernalillo, New Mexico, on Route 25. The caravan consists of Joseph and myself riding in a vintage gold Cadillac convertible with the top down, followed by several vans filled with program participants. Soon, a few drops of rain begin to fall. There were only a few large drops at first. Suddenly the sky opens and empties itself in a monsoon-like deluge. Rain pours down in blinding sheets drenching everything in sight—except or the two persons sitting in the convertible.

At first, I didn't even notice anything unusual about a torrential downpour without so much as a drop on us. Joseph and I were totally absorbed in conversation, talking excitedly about upcoming programs with ideas flowing back and forth. Not being rained on seemed almost natural. It was an extended moment in time when outer and inner worlds converged in a unified field. And whenever exceptionally inspired thoughts were expressed, claps of thunder resounded in agreement. The van directly behind us witnessed the Cadillac mystery. Karen, one of the passengers, described it this way:

> We all hear the loud thunder and watch as a heavy rain follows. We are amazed that the Cadillac continues to ride with its top down. We are very curious. Aren't they going to pull over and put the top up? Everyone in the van is watching this same surrealistic scene. The rain is not falling in the car. How can that be?
>
> We ask the van driver to pull a little closer to the Cadillac. What we witness is unimaginable. Invisible lines of demarcation at the front, back, sides, and top of the convertible totally block the rain from falling inside the car. We are stunned. We sit in silence, in disbelief. It is certainly a mystery, bur.t is it a miracle, or a trick of some kind? I would say I was seeing things were it not for the van full of people all witnessing the same extraordinary event.

Suddenly, my rational mind interrupted and began to question the situation. *No rain is falling on us!* The reality of this was startling. When cars passed, the occupants turned and looked in sheer disbelief at what they saw. Our convertible was dry. My long blonde hair was blowing freely in the breeze when it should have been saturated. They must have thought: *It can't be so, or can it?*

I turned around slightly and tried to look back with peripheral vision to see if the rear seat was dry. Joseph quickly redirected my attention, "Shh, don't say anything. It will break the spell." I immediately turned back around, eyes focused on the road ahead. We continued talking, and continued being shielded from the rain. It seemed like an experience out of a Fellini movie or a Castaneda book. Or was it a magical moment filled with grace when the cause-and-effect laws of this plane yield to higher laws. The downpour continued and our convertible top remained open. And we miraculously arrived at Bernalillo some forty-five minutes later bone-dry.

Normal and Paranormal Side by Side

Two days later, another paranormal experience occurred. This time I was with my son John. It all began in the morning when Joseph asked us to buy him a belt. The request was unusual. Knowing Joseph is not a material person, it seemed unlikely the request had anything to do with shopping in the usual context. Besides, Joseph has never asked me to buy him a gift.

So off we went shopping for a Native American belt in Taos where there is no scarcity of such items. We didn't have to look far to find hundreds of belts to choose from. A leather belt with fine beading quickly captured our attention making the selection process easy.

With the belt purchase taken care of, we decided to explore the area around Taos. We drove up to the D. H. Lawrence ranch to get a better understanding of the life and legacy of a gifted writer. Once we arrived at the ranch, we began walking on the grounds. Immediately a plump raccoon nimbly ambled down from a nearby tree and walked over to within five feet of us without any fear or hesitation. He looked directly at us for what seemed like a long time, as though he were sizing us up. In hindsight, the raccoon who is normally a nocturnal creature portends what is to come. *What you think you know is not what is. Expect the unexpected.*

After leaving the ranch, we drove to the Rio Grande gorge, a natural chasm created by erosion over many thousands of years. Peering down into the gorge is a rare peak into the belly of the earth. It is a breathtaking sight but no more spectacular than what we were about to witness.

Back on the road, some fifteen or twenty miles from the gorge, I gazed into an open field and was suddenly astonished. "John, are you seeing what

I'm seeing?" "You mean those two enormous columns of golden light?" "Yes." I was glad someone else was there to both affirm and share this experience.

In the field in front of us were two massive columns, two cylindrical circular shafts of light, each perhaps fifty feet in diameter and towering hundreds of feet tall. They seemed to emerge from the earth side by side and reach skyward as though dancing ever so subtly in place, all the while reflecting the golden light of the afternoon sun and shimmering with their own luminescence. We pulled to the side of the road so we could stare in amazement. There was silence. An eerie calm. No cars on the road. Everything which might have been distracting disappeared allowing us to totally absorb the moment. How long we stayed transfixed I do not know, for such moments cannot be measured in linear time.

When we arrived back in Bernalillo late afternoon, we gave Joseph the belt. He seemed pleased and immediately recognized the intricate beadwork on the belt as that done at Picuris, something we were not aware of when selecting it. Joseph then disclosed the real reason for the belt: it is a metaphor for peace. For some time thereafter, Joseph wore the belt in ceremonies and dances as a way to carry peace for *the people,* meaning the vibration of the greater whole.

I mentioned to Joseph that we had a most remarkable day. "Yeah, I thought it might be special," he replied calmly. When I described the two enormous whirling globes we had seen, Joseph answered in a very matter-of-fact tone, "They are the beings of the Land welcoming you."

And then again perhaps there is only entering and leaving that makes up the Totality of life. And Entering is really giving and Leaving is receiving.

By Beatrice Painted APRew
4/April/90

Inspired on this day by Mary Elizabeth Marlow

The Greater Reality

More and more I was *learning that behind everything in the physical reality, there is a greater spiritual reality.* Thus, a Sun Dancer dances to the sun, but he is really dancing to the spiritual light, the divine intelligence for which the sun is an extant metaphor. So the sun is not just the sun or the moon is not just the moon, and the nighttime not just the nighttime, for each physical reality represents something transcendent. Likewise, the belt and the raccoon had their messages to convey.

And paranormal experiences, such as rain being held back and shimmering columns of light, are sacred moments when we glimpse a greater reality. My perception was shifting as familiar and comfortable forms were deconstructed and as the very lens through which I perceived *reality* was reconfigured from narrow focus to wide angle. Many more experiences with the transcendent realm would occur during my years of walking with Joseph. I was learning again and again *what we think we know is not what is,* for *perceptual reality is in a state of impermanence and therefore is always changing.*

Experiences with the seemingly miraculous are seldom repeated. Perhaps we are to glimpse an expanded view of the nature of reality and learn what we can from these moments. However, exhilarating as they may be, having experiences such as these is not the primary goal. Nevertheless, they *grace* us with beauty and peace and show us the unity of life and the oneness of existence. They are forms which take us to a place beyond form.

> *I was born, I believe with a responsibility to assist people to rediscover their own personal songs, and therefore by singing together, we will all reconnect ourselves to divine presence here on Mother Earth for World Peace*
>
> — JOSEPH RAEL (BEAUTIFUL PAINTED ARROW)

CHAPTER NINE

LIVE INSIDE DIVINE PRESENCE

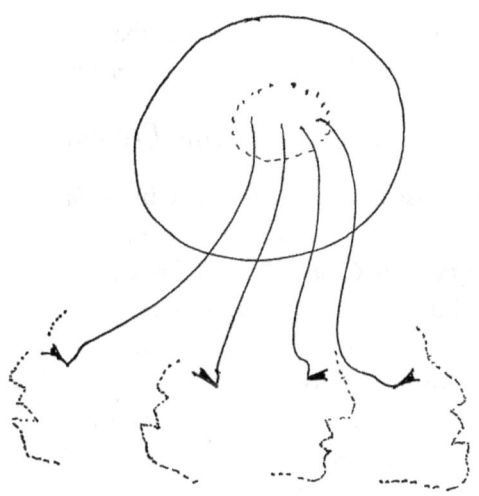

All that Exists is the Eternal Now

Many of the programs Joseph and I taught (vision quests, sacred sites and ceremonies, rites of passage, thunder calling, mysteries of the dance, metaphoric mind and others) took place outside. Once, when we were in a natural setting, Joseph placed each person so they were beyond the visible range of anyone else. Everyone had his or her private space. They were to sit in the center of an imaginary circle and *be present* in the center of their mind. From the center of that circle are four directions, four distinct corridors of the mind: the East (mental), South (emotional), West (physical), and North (spiritual).

After sitting for one hour facing each direction, they were to return to the direction they faced when they started and continue to sit for another hour. They sat alone in stillness, in hushed, pregnant silence and listened and paid close attention to every movement, form, color and sound and to every feeling, sensation, insight and realization. Carlos Castaneda's Don Juan referred to this state of being acutely aware as *mindfulness*.

When they returned to the direction they faced three hours earlier, there were of course noticeable differences in the light, shadows, and colors of the sky and landscape from that which they experienced earlier. The contrast, however, was greatly enhanced by their heightened state of awareness. An experience such as this may be simple, yet it translates powerful teachings at a visceral level in a way that words alone cannot: *Everything is impermanent. All that exists is the eternal now.*

Living inside Divine Presence

Being mindful is essential if one is to live in *Divine Presence*. Joseph once said: *I live inside vibrations made of divine presence every day and night so I will not ever be far from my Creator.* Such a far-reaching statement may be more than many of us can imagine or aspire to, yet we long for more of the Divine and long to be closer to that Presence.

According to a story from Joseph's tradition: *In the beginning there was One Being. Two fawns, a brother and sister, separated from the One Being went in two different directions and settled in two different places. One fawn settled in the realm of spirit; the other fawn settled in the realm of the material.*

The two fawns, of course, aren't real but are metaphors which represent two different perceptual realities which co-exist simultaneously. We may live primarily in one of these realities or shift frequently back and forth from one perspective to the other. When we abide in spirit, we live in loving Divine Presence. This is the place where we rediscover our *soul song*, our unique soul attributes, gifts and talents we have come here to express. The other perceptual reality is the material realm, where ego is driven by consensus reality and by individual, family, and generational patterns and beliefs. The question becomes: How can we live more of our lives abiding in Spirit? The most obvious answer has already been given. As often and as much as we can, we strive to live in the stillness of the moment, *in the eternal now.*

Divine Presence in the Creative

An artist friend of mind says that while growing up in New York City, his church, his sanctuary, was the Metropolitan Museum of Art. Early in life, he learned that creativity keeps one connected to the Creator. Now, many years later, his sanctuary is his studio. Not surprisingly, his paintings are inspired works, filled with Divine Presence. And it is not a surprise that most Native Americans honor the importance of creative energy and do something creative every day. For Joseph, it is drawing and painting. Others express in weaving, throwing pots, beading, jewelry-making or some other artistic form.

In 1988, through a series of synchronistic events, I was gifted with a trip to India by a most generous European lady who many affectionately call the Global Mother. She is the actor-behind-the-scenes who first brought the Dalai Lama to Europe, helped organize numerous international conferences, trips, meetings, gatherings, happenings around the world, and even provided an apartment in London for me and a host of others whenever we were teaching and needed a place to recharge. Upon arrival, the doorman would take our baggage and open the door of a lovely, freshly cleaned apartment with a refrigerator well-stocked with food. It made teaching in London not only a privilege but a joy!

As if that was not enough, the Global Mother generously invited me, as a guest, to join a month-long spiritual pilgrimage throughout India with twelve women: three Americans and nine Europeans. Our journey included everything from a retreat on Mount Abu (location of the Brahma Kumaris), to the ashram of Sai Baba (where thousands gathered to receive his blessing, to Auroville and the Sri Aurobindo Community, and to the Motherhouse in Calcutta (home of Mother Teresa and the Missionaries of Charity.)

One of the pilgrims on this trip was the late acclaimed Dutch artist, Diana Vandenberg. We became close friends during our travels together. Diana said of herself, "I am an artist. Everything I do connects me to art, whether that is travel, physics, or the literature I read. Art is the one river in my life and everything connects and flows into that river. I paint every day whether I want to or not. When I am not in an especially creative space, I do the detail work. When I am in a more creative space, I allow inspiration to guide."

Meeting someone with a clear commitment to art is inspiring. I wondered how the world looked through her eyes. Life offered the perfect opportunity to answer that question. We agreed to forgo the bus ride back to our hotel. Instead we would take a three mile walk together in a rural Indian landscape. Would she be willing to share whatever might draw her attention along the way? For I was curious as to what her eyes would notice. Diana graciously agreed.

During our walk together, she intermittently described in detail her perceptions: the ancient, pensive, world-weary eyes of a little boy as he walked past with his mother; the delight in discovering an exquisite red flower reaching its head out from behind a rock; the beguiling perfume of a mango tree laden with delicate fruit juxtaposed with an extraordinarily ugly beetle crawling on one of its leaves; and the subtle color gradations of browns and greys in the parched earth, otherwise uninteresting until Diana made them intriguing.

Divine Presence in Spiritual Practices and Disciplines

A universally accepted way to be in Divine Presence is through spiritual practices and disciplines. The practices themselves are as varied as the traditions they represent. Whether it be through sacred texts and scriptures, prayers, meditation, rituals or yoga, they hold in common an understanding that spiritual practices kindle the light within and keep one unified and centered in the Divine. Joseph engages in many spiritual practices which are an integral part of his life, be it prayer, meditation, fasting, chanting, ceremonial dancing, vision questing on a mountainside, sweat lodge ceremonies, pilgrimage to Chimayo, and working with the medicine wheel.

Divine Presence in Nature

Santa Fe Summer © 2010 John S. Atkinson
Hampton Roads Giclee info@hrgiclee.com

Joseph describes himself as basically a *nature boy* because he spent much of his childhood and still spends much of his adult life outdoors. Nature connects us not only with the natural world but with the natural self. Many people find their sanctuary in nature. Some choose careers which keep them outdoors. Others make quiet discoveries while working in their garden or walking through unfamiliar woods, or in the awe of watching the sun spread its rays through the overcast sky. In those sacred moments we unite with the wonderment and beauty of the Divine.

Divine Presence in Serving Others

Dr. Elizabeth Kubler Ross, preeminent psychiatrist and pioneer in exploring the stages of death and dying, once said that she did not meditate. However, if meditation includes sitting by the bedside while someone is dying, then she had spent many hours doing just that. A response such as this reminds us that we can never be too quick to judge how someone else keeps their spiritual connection. Hers was a particular path of service and there are an infinite number of ways to be of selfless service to other—everything from random acts of kindness to entire lives dedicated to serving others.

It is in losing our self that we find our true self, for in giving to others, we lose our egocentricity and open to the Higher Self. Perhaps it matters not *how* we stay connected to Spirit only that, as often as we can, we find a way to live connected to the Divine.

Spiritual Gifts

When we live in Divine Presence, Higher Mind is expressed in an infinite numbers of ways. One of these ways is through the many spiritual gifts which can be used in service to others. As cosmic dancers, we are in the process of remembering latent domains of consciousness. By opening to the Divine, we recover these potentials and reclaim them.

During my first visit to the Sound/Peace Chamber I became aware of two of Joseph's gifts. One of those is giving Spirit Names which capture the unique soul essence of a person and serve to connect that person to the current phase of their life. When Joseph *names*, he becomes still, listens within, and conveys what he is told. During a particular sacred sites program he gave the name *Red Arrow* to one man, not knowing he was about to open a courier service with this very same name. Another group member was given the name *Blue Butterfly*.

When asked why that particular name, Joseph responded, *I am going to tell you a creation story. In the beginning God created the world, the air, earth, water, and all the animals. The first animal he made was the blue butterfly so she could flutter her wings and use them like a paintbrush. That name is given so you can color everything as you wish.*

Unknown to Joseph, this person not only has a special affinity for butterflies, but is an artist. She decided thereafter to name her gallery *Blue Butterfly* because the name struck such a resonant chord with her.

During another time when our group had gathered high up in the mountains, we took a break and Joseph started giving Spirit Names to everyone. Joseph noticed the young man sitting under a tree drawing. Joseph casually said, *Tell Michael to come over here. He needs a name.* Michael immediately got up and walked over to Joseph who stood silent for a moment and then said, *You are White Cloud, who is often in the mind of God.* With that, thunder rolled across the sky. *If you should ever forget who you are, look up to the clouds and you will remember.* Again thunder rolled louder than before, even though the cloudless Sky was blue and serene.

A Second Gift

It became apparent during the original Sound/Peace Chamber experience that Joseph is a healer, although he would be the first to say that *he* doesn't do anything. *I just work here,* is how he explains it. Again, as with naming, he listens within and does what he is told.

One of the seven participants who had come to open the Sound/Peace Chamber had a severe skin rash. First, Joseph took his eagle feather and cleared her energy with a few graceful strokes of the feather. He then told her he was going to *blow his breath through the top of her head.* She could feel him blow breath into her heart. Almost immediately she became so cold she felt as though she was lying on ice. The incessant itching from the rash stopped and within three days it was gone entirely.

There are many examples of different types of healing I witnessed over the years. During a Drum Dance, one of the female dancers began experiencing severe back pain. Joseph quietly walked up behind her, placed his eagle feather on her back. As soon as the feathers touched her back, her pain was immediately gone.

With cancer patients, Joseph listens to the cancer to hear whether it is a running cancer, a sitting cancer or a standing cancer. According to the kind of cancer he hears, he then uses the specific sound which is the antidote for that type of cancer.

On yet another occasion, a woman Joseph had never met came to Bernalillo for a healing session. While they were in the Sound/Peace Chamber, a strong vortex of wind and energy started swirling around the top of the chamber. I don't know what her ailment was though I do know the outer landscape affirmed a powerful energy exchange. Later, Joseph commented that working with her was like being with a medicine woman.

Once when an overnight guest in my home took ill, what began as his gnawing discomfort soon turned into excruciating abdominal pain. We were preparing to head to a nearby emergency facility when coincidentally Joseph telephoned and I mentioned the condition of the person staying with me.

Joseph said to put a small clipping of cedar under a glass of water and then my friend should drink the water. No cedar grows around my home. So instead of going to the emergency room, we got in the car on that snowy night, riding up and down streets in search of cedar, which we finally located. We cut off a small clipping. Rational? Not at all. I had learned early on from my experiences with Joseph that the linear mind is valuable and has its place. Higher Mind works differently.

We returned home and placed the cedar under the glass as directed for a few minutes, so the water could absorb its healing properties. My friend then drank the water. The pain soon subsided. He then developed an appetite enough to take some nourishment, an impossibility only a few hours earlier. The cedar opens us to higher worlds. Water is Light. These were the catalysts which, in metaphor, helped make the necessary shift in his consciousness.

Healing the Past

During a sweat lodge ceremony, Lynne, a long-time friend and one of the participants, came out of the sweat lodge sobbing and gasping for breath. Joseph said, "What's happening?"

"I don't know. I feel overwhelmed, emotionally."

"Come with me." He walked her into the nearby Sound/ Peace Chamber, where he sat her in a chair surrounded by piles of sagebrush. She was immediately enveloped in the sweet, soothing smell of the sage.

"How old are you?" Joseph asked. "Fifty-eight."

"I am going to count backwards and take you back year by year." The aroma of sage seemed to help transport her back in time. When he got to year one, Joseph said, "Now I am going to count backwards from twelve months to one month." He stopped at six months, for again, there were sobs and old tears. The anxiety and labored breathing returned as Lynne began to relive an episode she experienced at six months old in which her lungs collapsed from pneumonia. In her reverie, she regressed to her infancy: The family doctor was present, for it was a time when doctors still made house calls. She saw herself as a little baby turning blue and knew she was suffocating and experiencing the same feelings that were activated in the sweat lodge. The doctor thumped on her back and finally she began to breathe again.

Joseph continued to count backwards, "Five, four, three, two, one . . . Now you are in your mother's womb. What do you feel?" "I feel sad."

"You are picking up on your mother's sadness. What is she sad about?"

"She is sad about her father's death."

"You carry your mother's sadness. Now see yourself coming out of the womb and being born. What do you see?" "I see light."

Her anxiety was gone and her breath steady. "I remember my mother saying, 'You are the light of my life'." It makes me feel good to remember that."

"Now I am going to count you back up to fifty-eight."

After the healing ceremony, Lynne returned to the group with a renewed sense of self.

"Holographic Universe"

About ninety percent of Joseph's healings are done remotely at a distance. We know from physics that our mind is nonlocal, an extended awareness not limited by time and space. Physicist David Bohm describes this interconnectedness as a "holographic universe" in which everything is connected to and reflective of everything else, a truth the Buddha knew from direct experience: "Separation is illusion."

There is no difference in whether a healing is done in person or whether we hold that person in our thoughts from a distance. The impact is the same. When healing from a distance, Joseph sometimes *sends* what he describes as a *ball of light*. The recipients of that light feel its power.

In addition to the gifts of healing and naming, Joseph's visionary capacities are remarkable. As a cosmic dancer he moves in an out of different realities bringing insights and visions for the collective.

We may not develop the ability to give spiritual names or heal in the same way as does Joseph or be a visionary. That is not our goal, and we are not result-oriented. What we can do is establish an intention to *live more and more in Divine Presence so we are never far from our Creator.* When we do this, we express the highest and noblest aspects of our being. We are given whatever spiritual capacities and gifts are needed for the particular task at hand. And as we use these gifts in service to others, they are enhanced.

CHAPTER TEN

FALL IN LOVE WITH LIFE

Expect the Unexpected

DURING THE DRUM DANCE AT POTTSTOWN IN JUNE 2007, I was inspired to write this book. My focus turned to Joseph, to the various experiences and stories we shared and the insights learned along the way. Though there was no plan as to how those teachings would coalesce, as soon as the dance was over, the writing began in my usual unorganized, organic way. Rather than working from an outline (the usual method of writing) I love the *not knowing*, the surrender to emptiness, the waiting and listening to what bubbles up from deep within. The nine chapters became self-evident. Once the themes were revealed, I would often wake up in the early morning recalling the precise stories and experiences needed to illustrate and weave together what was being written. Thus, writing the first nine chapters was effortless.

The tenth last chapter was a mystery and presented me with writer's block. Maybe I had not fully absorbed and integrated this ten year journey enough to continue. In addition, there were new challenges to meet. More time and space, more deep seeing and listening were required. So rather than force something, the book was put on pause for what became a long interlude—and my attention went elsewhere.

The number ten has many derivatives. In the Biblical tradition, ten means man walking with God. We neither lag and walk behind God nor rush and walk ahead of God. Instead, we walk with Him and proceed with right timing and right action. And suddenly in 2016, I woke up one morning knowing it was time to fine-tune what had been written and complete the tenth and last chapter.

The Innocent Accepts What Is

I began to reflect on the ten-year sojourn with Joseph, beginning with our first silent meeting on a wooded path in Virginia Beach. This encounter was a reminder that first impressions are often both true and lasting. For it was in that auspicious moment that Joseph appeared as one of the ancient ones who had merged with the heart of God.

And some years later when meeting Joseph in Bernalillo where he lived near the train tracks in a humble trailer adjacent to the Sound/Peace Chamber . . . it was again evident that this simple, wise man was *an innocent, ever aware of the beauty and great mystery of life*. He was then and continues to be always and eternally, someone who is *in love with life*. That, then, would be the obvious theme for chapter ten.

What Does the Moment Ask?

So how does one stay innocent, ever open to what life presents regardless of circumstances? Perhaps a clue can be found in the following story. Prior to the start of a retreat we lead some years ago, participants from various parts of the U.S. and Europe were to meet at the Albuquerque airport and then car-caravan to Durango.

I rode ahead with one group. Joseph was riding in a car with a different group which was followed by cars filled with still other groups. Less than halfway to our destination, the car behind Joseph's developed engine trouble, first spurting out fumes, then making strange noises and finally dying altogether. Aware of what was happening, Joseph asked the driver of his car to stop and see if they could be of any assistance.

According to Russell, who was the driver of the broken-down rented vehicle, the problem seemed serious, not easy to fix. Maybe the car needs to be towed. If that happens, then Joseph would arrive late at the seminar and maybe even miss the evening session altogether. Knowing that people had traveled a long way to hear Joseph speak, Russell suggested Joseph go with another car.

"People have traveled a long way to hear what you have to say this evening. So go on ahead. We'll take care of the car."

Joseph's early Tiwa training taught him to silently pose only one pertinent question: what does the moment ask? The *moment* asked him to help fix the car, which he did. So Joseph can also fix cars when needed? Good to know. No blame, no judgment, no frustration, no worry. His only response was, "I guess I wasn't supposed to be where I thought I was," referring to his scheduled lecture in Durango. It seems how we deal with the little things in life often mirror the way we confront more challenging situations.

An hour later, both groups were happily back on the road again, making it possible for everyone to arrive in time for the evening session. *Everything is the way it is supposed to be* . . . a helpful lesson to remember.

The Innocent Avoids Blaming

On the first night of one particular vision quest, a few rain drops began to fall, gently at first, as though the sky was deciding whether to just sprinkle the earth or create a downpour of heavy rain. I suddenly realized that information about rain gear had not been included in the letter sent to the participants. Many of the participants were seasoned campers and had packed appropriately. Those from Europe, however, had packed lightly because of airplane restrictions and were not fully equipped.

The rain became more intense. I went to Joseph and told him about the situation. He was totally unmoved with the news. There was no blame or criticism about my inattention to detail. Instead of saying anything about the oversight, Joseph remained totally in harmony with the moment and remarked calmly, "What we need is some wind to come up from the West and move these clouds away. I will ask the grandfathers."

Not many of us could respond that way. For Joseph, communication with the grandfathers is quite natural, nothing extraordinary. So dressed in his usual simple attire (jeans, plaid flannel shirt, and baseball cap) and with no drama of any kind to call attention to himself, he said nothing and sat looking straight ahead in silent, Buddha-like stillness. As for the campers, they were never told this story. They just assumed the rain stopped on its own.

Falling in Love with Life

According to Joseph, the key to falling in love with life is *to avoid blame*. This includes unconstructive criticism, judging, or censorship of any kind. When we blame, we separate ourselves from others and make ourselves out to be superior, better, different, inferior, lesser, or helpless. When we lose our innocence, we lose our ability to listen to Higher Mind who infuses us with infinite possibilities. A teaching is ours only when we can apply it in our lives. Therefore, until we can demonstrate or live that teaching, it is just borrowed second-hand information.

The innocent *accepts what is and* seeks only *what the moment asks* are important constructs in everyday situations. They are more relevant when we are faced with extremely challenging experiences, such as natural disaster, disturbing health news, incarceration, betrayal, or tragic loss of any kind. Life teaches us there is really no good or bad moment, no particular experience *better or worse* than another. Any moment, any experience *is* really *a divine happening*, a potential initiation to the next epiphany.

With any crisis, we can learn to embrace and accept the challenge life presents and find the gift it brings. How else would we be able to plunge to new depths of awareness? How else could we fully realize the blessing that is our family and friends and experience new levels of intimacy, vulnerability, and trust? How else could we develop a deeper understanding and compassion for the physical, emotional and mental challenges millions suffer and endure each day? Life presents us with wake-up calls and reminds us to shake off *old stuff*. We can pause and enter the unknown with childlike wonder.

During this inward journey, it was also helpful to reflect on friends who had been challenged and yet remained innocent, in love with the beauty and mystery of life. A couple in Holland comes to mind, a doctor and his wife, who became pregnant with their fourth child rather late in life. There was some concern during the pregnancy that the unborn baby was not moving very much, as this is a possible indicator of Down syndrome. When amniocentesis was suggested to check for this condition, the parents' answer was clear: "No need to do that. Whatever happens, we will take this child and we will love this child."

Likewise, when my longtime friend from Texas sums up her many arduous years of misdiagnoses, evasive answers, and often experimental treatments for her now adult child with special needs. It is not pain and hardship that is her focus. Instead, the smile on her face and her heartfelt words say it all: "This life lesson has been my greatest opportunity for growth. I would not have had it any other way."

An Innocent Gives to Others

As I reflect on the ten years with Joseph, I am reminded of the many random, generous gestures which brought light and joy to the receiver. Three very different examples of goodness come to mind.

Copper Medicine

It was New Year's Eve 1999. Like many others, we were excited and expectant about the clock rolling over to the year 2000. It seemed somewhat unreal. As a planet we were about to enter another chapter in our journey. As a people, we could choose to live our greater story and open to infinite possibilities.

Much to my surprise, I received a late phone call from Joseph. (As mentioned before, Joseph is not a telephone person. He calls if there is something important to share, otherwise not). I was delighted to hear from him. His message was memorable:

> It is New Years' Eve and we are about to enter another era. I just want you to know that I have buried a copper medicine piece in the Sangria Mountains. I know you travel a great deal. So if you ever get tired, know you can draw on the energy of the copper. It will strengthen you.

I was deeply touched with his thoughtfulness. So, afterwards, whenever I was weary and jet lagged, I would visualize cooper buried in the mountains and somehow feel renewed.

As to the broader significance of copper, I have learned since that for thousands of years, the Egyptians knew copper to be a healing component. A memory came to mind of a friend sharing her experience of wearing a copper bracelet which seemed to heal her tennis elbow. Now, copper is even recognized as an important element in preventing the spread of bacteria. In fact, at the Virginia Beach Sentara Leigh Hospital, considered a leading-edge orthopedic center for leg and hip replacement, the bed sheets and surfaces of counter tops contain copper. No doubt the Native people knew about the healing properties of copper many years ago. We are just now discovering its importance. What a unique and beautiful gift to begin a new era.

Spirit Name

A friend asked Dee to go with her to a Long Dance which Joseph had originally established in New Mexico and then passed on to trained students. Having listened to the stories about Joseph and his teachings for years, Dee was very excited to join her. She tells the story this way . . .

"Upon arrival, we were asked to set an individual intention for our Dance which would be added to the group intention of World Peace. Having just undergone some major changes in my life: a divorce after 30 years of marriage, termination of a long held job, a move to a new city, and the loss of a beloved pet, I wanted to mark this transition with a new name. The initials to my name I had always answered to just didn't seem to fit any more. During the weekend, people continually offered suggestions. None of them felt right.

Before the start of the dance, we all gathered for final instruction. As we sat waiting, Joseph suddenly appeared in the doorway. He had been traveling and the dance location was on his way home. It was a spur of the moment decision to stop by. Even the dance organizers were surprised.

An even bigger surprise was when Joseph called us up individually and gave us our Spirit Names. Until then, I only knew two people who had received their Spirit Names. Never in my wildest dreams did I believe I would have one of my own. The name given me was *Sunrise*. How appropriate, since for about a year I had been getting up early every morning to watch the sun rise over the ocean.

The wonders didn't stop there. Two weeks after the dance, an e-mail from the organizers came with an order form to purchase a Joseph drawing of my Spirit Name. Having admired Joseph's drawing for years, there was no question: Yes! I do want a Spirit Name drawing.

Soon afterwards, I noticed a voice message from an unknown caller on my cell phone. The message was from Joseph and it went something like this: "*I started to draw your name and these rain people started dropping out of the sky. So your name is Sunrise and Raining Light.*"

I kept this message on my phone for a very long time. I had asked for a new name and received a much more valuable Spirit Name instead. It was a reminder of Joseph's caring answer to my heartfelt prayers and the magic and power of the dance."

You Called?

John was born an animal lover. More than once he had nursed birds back to life. Once he even rescued a frozen duck from a river and somehow managed to bring life back to one very lucky duck. In particular, though, he loved dogs of every species and variety.

So it came as no surprise that when our group of participants arrived and everyone was seated in a circle, John casually mentioned his wish to see a coyote while he was in New Mexico. Joseph just happened to hear the conversation.

When John had his first opportunity to drive one of the vans filed with our participants down New Mexico's highway, Joseph spotted a coyote in the distance. Joseph told him to turn the van around so he could see him better. John got a quick glance and then the coyote had another agenda, for he quickly scurried out of sight. Nevertheless, John had indeed seen a genuine coyote!

A few days later, Joseph unexpectedly said, "Come on, John, Let's go up there, pointing to a hill. I am going to teach you how to call in a coyote." So off they went—John at 6 feet 7 and Joseph a 5 feet 6—the long and short of it going off together.

The deep seeing and deep listening Joseph learned as a child is entrenched in his psyche and is who he is. When appropriate, those gifts can be taught to another . . . as John was about to learn. When they returned, Joseph said, "We didn't have much time and I think it was just enough."

I didn't ask John what happened nor did he offer any information. After all, this was 'man stuff'. John was deeply grateful. It was of those rare peak experiences you want to savor . . . how many people get the opportunity to have a shaman individually teach you how to call in coyotes? And that was that. . . . or was it?

Our group of participants stayed in a cluster of small rented adobes in downtown Santa Fe. Each pueblo had a living room, two bedrooms, small kitchen and a deck. That evening I went to bed early. John, as usual, sat comfortably in a chair on the deck drawing into the wee hours. Suddenly, I was awakened from a deep sleep when John came rushing into my room. "Mom, mom, you won't believe what is on the deck." His heart was pounding with excitement.

I quickly jumped out of bed and rushed to the windows staring with awe. There standing before us were three coyotes situated on the very small 5 by 7 deck. One looked directly at us with piercing eyes as if to say, 'You called? We heard your call and we are here! Now, what?'

More On The Way

My friend Russell once said to Joseph, "I wish there were more people like you." Without missing a beat, Joseph answered, "There are more on the way."

The *more* does not need to be the next generation. It is potentially you, me, any of us, and all of us. We are all in the process of becoming the cosmic dancers we are destined to be, open to spiritual capacities and spiritual gifts, fed by the invisible dimensions which enliven us and infuse us with light.

When we fall in love with life, we remember who we are. Our 'little self' dissolves and we regain our innocence. We listen to our own personal song. We are teachable, excited about the possibilities of each day, the next insight, the discovery of the next mystery. We are creative, alive, loving, and knowing.

We open to the Vast Self... the Cosmic Dancer who is informed and danced by Higher Mind.

NOTES

PROLOGUE : REMARKABLE MEETING

Rael, Joseph and Marlow, Mary Elizabeth. *Being & Vibration.* Tulsa, Oklahoma: Council Oak Books, 1993. Introduction, p. 1.

CHAPTER ONE : LISTENING IS GIVING

Wilhelm, Richard and Baynes, Cary F. *The I Ching or Book of Changes.* Princeton, New Jersey: Princeton University Press, 1967. When teaching the subject of intuition, Paul Solomon referred to the principle of the first, second and third son from the I Ching to explain the intuitive process. I wrote my memory of that teaching.

Rael, Joseph and Marlow, Mary Elizabeth. *Being & Vibration.* Tulsa, Oklahoma: Council Oak Books, 1993. p. 29–32.

CHAPTER TWO : METAPHORS ARE THE LANGUAGE OF UNIVERSAL CONSCIOUSNESS

Rael, Joseph and Marlow, Mary Elizabeth, *Being & Vibration.* Tulsa, Oklahoma: Council Oak Books, 1990, p.124.

CHAPTER THREE : ALL CEREMONIES GET US IN TOUCH WITH HIGHER MIND

Campbell, Joseph in conversation with Michael Tom. *An Open Life.* New York, New York: Harper & Row, 1989, p.26.

Mullaney, James. *Edgar Cayce and the Cosmos.* Virginia Beach, Virginia: ARE Press, 2007. p. 9–13.

CHAPTER SIX : WE ARE NOT HERE

Josephy, Jr., Alvin M. *500 Nations: An Illustrated History of North American Indians,* New York, New York: Alfred A. Knope, 1994. p. 157.

Braden, Greg. *The Divine Matrix.* Carlsbad, California: Hay House, Inc., 2007. p.23–24.

Katon, Jane, Ph, D. and Targ, Russell,. *The Heart of the Mind: How to Experience God Without Belief.* Novata, California. New World Library, 1999, p.57.

Stopinder, A Gurdjieff. *Journal For Our Time,* number 6, fall 2001, p. 41–43. An interview with Joseph Rael, conducted by Ben Hitchner which includes material on Joseph's work with a group of scientists concerned with quantum linguistics.

CHAPTER SEVEN : DON'T GET STUCK IN FORM

Solstice Shift: Magical Blend's Synergistic Guide to the Coming Age, edited by John Nelson. A series of commentaries by well-known authors on the transformative shift in consciousness. Jean Houston points to *The New Myths of our Time*. Charlottesville, Virginia; Hampton Roads Publishing, 1997, p. 154.

Kamenetz, Rodger. *The Jew in the Lotus: A Poet's Rediscovery of Jewish Identity in Buddhist India*. San Francisco, California; Harper San Francisco, 1994, p.2, 3.

CHAPTER NINE : LIVE INSIDE DIVINE PRESENCE

Holy Bible (New Revised Standard Version) John 14:26

Katan, Jane, PhD and Targ, Russell. *How to Experience God Without Belief*. Novata, California: New World Library, 1999. p.15.

CHAPTER TEN : FALL IN LOVE WITH LIFE

The Wisdom of Solomon (Paul Solomon). Compiled and Edited by Grace de Rond, Printed in the USA; 2010, p.455, 456.

ACKNOWLEDGEMENTS

First and foremost, thank you, Joseph Rael (Beautiful Painted Arrow), for your permission and blessing in writing this book. I am also grateful to a wonderful group of people who encouraged, supported and gave valuable commentary as *Walking With a Cosmic Dancer Joseph Rael* went through its metamorphosis. In the early version, Dee Keller, Lynne Paine, and Karen Vermillion were particularly helpful. In addition to being my trusted friends, they helped me express the goodness and unique wisdom Joseph brings to every experience.

Helpful in a different way were three other women: Arleen Cohen, Joy Bloom, and Ronnie Kochey, who draw from Buddhist, Jungian and rich life experiences. Because they have never known Joseph, they brought a totally objective view. They made certain the teachings were clear enough for the reader to absorb and make useful in their lives. Many thanks also to those persons who were willing to share their stories. They allow others to travel alongside and partake in amazing happenings which shift perceptions and open us to Higher Mind and infinite possibilities.

After a ten year wait period, a second group of helpers arrived to complete this book. Stephen Haslam a long-time friend, provided a professional overview and analysis which was extremely helpful. Maggie Courtier arrived on the scene to bring her skills of careful editing. Thanks also to Linda Berardi and Michele Fink for graciously providing the photographs which help tell the stories.

I am especially thankful for Dee Keller. She continually insisted on more when I might have settled for less. Her intuition, clarity, and esthetic sensitivity were much appreciated. She was particularly helpful in making the artistic decisions in designing and formatting. Dee was taught by Joseph and participated in ceremonies and retreats lead by him. Thus, she not only brought her first-hand experiences on board but a deep longing to present Joseph's teachings.

Above all others, I am grateful to my son, the late John S. Atkinson. Not only did I have the joy of sharing mutual experiences with him (some of which are included in the book) but also the pleasure of working with him as the primary assistant author. Not only does John write beautifully but he also has a delightful zen quality. In that space, he is the *cosmic dancer* who is danced by Higher Mind and perceives with an awareness which is clear and insightful. My deep gratitude.

And finally, I thank the Great Mystery that brought an unlikely pair together. It gave me the opportunity to experience a transformative journey full of challenge, ecstasy, and a memorable glimpse into the heart of a mystic.

ABOUT THE AUTHOR

Mary Elizabeth Marlow is the author of *Jumping Mouse: A Story about Inner Trust*, *Handbook for the Emerging Woman*, and her new book entitled *Walking with Cosmic Dancer Joseph Rael*. Her books have been translated in seven languages: Spanish, German, Turkish Hebrew, Norwegian, French, Korean and Portuguese. In addition, she has been featured in international magazines including *New Woman*, *Live Lyst*, *Human Potential*, *Libellee*, *Onkruid*, and *Hjemmet*.

She has spoken to a wide range of audiences including: 1990 International Peace Conference (the Hague) Mythic Journey Conference(Atlanta), Whole Life Expo (New York and Los Angeles), Woman and Power Conference(London), Association for Research and Enlightenment (Virginia Beach), Center for Recovering Families (Houston), Festival of Mind, Body and Spirit (London), International Day of the Woman (Madrid), the Academy of Medicine (Amsterdam), and the Nidaros-Fonder, the Medical Congress in Trondheim, Norway. She has had some 60 teaching trips to Europe.

Mary Elizabeth co-taught for thirteen years with the late Paul Solomon, an international teacher who created a course intitled Inner Light Consciousness, ILC. Not only was Paul a gifted speaker but his teachings on meditation, spiritual journaling and dreams opened the doors to others who wanted to travel and teach ILC world-wide. A later experience, and one quite different, was ten years co-teaching and learning from mystic and visionary Joseph Rael. As a story-teller, it was a treasured gift for me to step into an ancient world where stories can be gathered along the way.

Important also were the thirty years co-teaching many seminars and retreats for women with my Texas friend, Lynne Paine M.E.D. LPC. Locations for the retreats included places like Galveston, Texas, Santa Fe,

New Mexico, and Hydra, Greece. Topics for the retreats varied such as: *Release Your Fire*: boldly claim your gifts, *Changing Woman*: a wise woman asks herself what do I keep? and what do I release? *Phoenix Rising*: a Greek Experience in transcending limitations: mold in clay the story you are now creating and make new choices. We listened to each person's story: their dreams, guided reveries, insights, myths, and spontaneous drawings. The take-away from the retreat programs offered deep bonds, joy, new horizons, waking up to what is soulful and true ... and transforming ones limited story to ones greater story.

This collage of happenings molded me to be author, inspirational speaker, and story teller based on my life experiences.

Memarlow9@cox.net

www.ingramcontent.com/pod-product-compliance
Lightning Source LLC
Chambersburg PA
CBHW062117080426
42734CB00012B/2895